SIXTEEN

SIXTEEN

With No Place to Call Home

RAYLENE WILLIAMS

InOtherWordzPublishing

To all my *Readers,*
I just want, to thank you for all your support.
To my *Parents*, I love you all!
S.I.P Dad Allen K. Hayman!
I told you I would become an author!
To my *Children,* you are the *INSPIRATION*
behind all I do.
Praying my story reaches every heart that
needs the messages that lie within.
Bringing families together everywhere.
I love you all
Smooches
Ravlene

I

Table OF Contents

1991

I remember it like it was yesterday,
The feelings are oh surreal. I had just got home from Tower mall.
My mom said, "Raylene we need to talk."
What was she going to say to me? I was so nervous,
This was it, I kept telling myself,
She is going to put me out. My heart was racing! An
An uncontainable eruption of emotions seemed to overtake me.
Mommy told me, that I was being kicked out.
I was no longer able to stay in her home.
Basically, she was tired of me and my mess. She was so done with
me and my behavior,
In a nutshell, she was tired of my shenanigans.
It was not a secret, that my mom wanted to release herself from
me. She completely wanted to be unattached.
All our family and friends knew, we bickered constantly.
They all knew that me and my mom,
Could never see eye to eye, when it came to anything. It was not
like this information was classified; she had made it known to every-
one that was around. People would tell me all the time "Your mom
doesn't want you living here anymore."
That was the main topic for conversation. She never valued my
point of view, so what was the purpose anyway I thought. She never
Wanted to hear anything I had to say. In her eyes, I was a child.
Not just the child, but the problem child.
According to her, I was sowing my wild oats, acting
Like my daddy's people. Some people I was never
Given the chance to know, at that time. I was never able to
Figure out how I could behave like people that I had never met
in my life.

My siblings all had the same parents that lived at home.

"They were blessed, to have both parents in the home."

She stated. Not me, I was a bastard child.

Born to parents that were not married, stated my mom when describing my birth. My mom was married to my stepdad, unlike the relationship she had with my father.

I didn't know whether I was a bastard or not, just figured I agreed since I was always

In some mess. It was possible I could actually be a bastard.

Well, that is until I looked up the definition to get a

Perception.

The definition of a bastard was of questionable origin, offensive person, and illegitimate. Not recognized as lawful offspring. So, I was labeled and put in a specific category with like folks. Not sure what she understood about people like me. She referenced, the Bible states that I would not enter the Congregation of the Lord.

This is how I was raised, like seriously, if that's the case, so I have to pay for my parents' sin. One that I did not commit, so being born was my punishment. They could be blessed, but I could not. Ok, sure something to that degree. I don't understand all that,

However, we all have views. Her view was based upon religious belief.

The circle of friends and other adults around did not see us

Having issues. They didn't even see us having communications problems.

What they saw was us

Not getting along and they all had opinions and I, Raylene, was the problem.

I grew up in a Christian home, with Pentecostal views. We weren't allowed to listen to secular music, wear pants or male garments. The Bible was used as a compass of rules which we believers must follow. My mom made sure if there was a kingdom, we surely

were going to get in. More like a guide to living a life respectable
and upright. We spent almost all

Our awake hours in church. Most of my friends I obtained, were
children

Of other church members.

There weren't to many secrets between us kids we knew each
other's business, we were nosey. They all knew my mom wasn't too
happy with me. They were having issues with their own parents.
Most of their parents all hated me. They were fake to me and follow-
ers, so I didn't care. They never said it, but they never had to It was
very apparent and I could tell by the way they treated me.

But wasn't this normal right?

For moms to get tired of their children's bad behavior. Is this the
protocol for bad behavior? Putting one's child out on the street to
face the world alone, this was the answer?

Parents always threaten things to their children when

They are mad, right? Keep it up and you are going to go live with
your

Grandparents. Or keep it up will end up living with your mom
or going to live with your dad.

These are usually threats

 Parents say to get a child to think about their behavior.

What, I wondered was what teen

Ever followed, all their parent's rules and directions?

I mean completely and without error?

My Family was far from normal and things

were about to get even more insane.

Too many things were going

On at one time. Trying to get a grip on life feeling

As if I was speeding on the highway.

Time was not waiting on me

To get my thoughts together either.

This was it this time no turning back, I was about to be,
On my own wandering through the universe.
As far back as I could remember I never think my mom liked me,
Not as a daughter or even as a person.
If she did, she had a ridiculously hard time showing the like.
I believe my very presence repulsed her to the core. I just
Knew that life had to be better than this.

QUESTIONS

Was I taught to love her? Will she ever love me? Is she my real mom? Who told her she had to keep me? Was abortion available? Was I adopted? What is going on for real? What happened that caused my existence? Was I planned or a mistake? Did my parents go out, did they even date? Are dads ok with just leaving kids with moms just because they're moms? Do dads know what is happening, to the children left behind? Do men have feelings? Are they capable of love? Do men really love their daughters?

Do dads only care about what happens to sons? Is someone/ anyone supposed to care? Where are my grandparents? Do they even care that I am here? Is this the definition of family? Am I going to be by myself forever? Will anyone ever like me for who I am? Will I ever find anyone on Earth to love me? Am I Dreaming? Where will I live? Whose idea was this anyway? Would I and my dad get along? Will he like me? Will I just be another burden?

Do I have a lot of aunts and uncles? What about cousins? Is my family big or small? Am I going to make new friends at my new school? Will I fit in? Can I really fight, like if I needed to protect myself, could I? Am I strong or confident? Is my face pretty? Would I get a boyfriend? What am I going to wear at my new school? What if my dad does not want me in his life? Does his family, even want to meet me?

Why am I so panicky? For what reason do I have to be frightened? Why do I feel so sad and unhappy? Is it normal to have this many questions? Why can't I just be perfect? Is life supposed to be this complicated? What am I missing here?

Why is mommy so mean, to mean? Who are the people who hurt her? Where are the people who hurt my mom? Were they punished for the injustice bestowed upon her? Are generational curses real?

Do I have talents? Am I good at anything? Will I have any good qualities in life? Does God really love me? IF so, why would he allow the mistreatment of Raylene? Why was I born? Why am I here? Is this some kind of joke? Who will I talk to? Better yet, who will Listen? Who cares? Who gives a fuck about me? Do I love; Raylene? Will I be like them as adults? Will I repeat what was done to me?

What does my Stepdad think? I think he likes me; does he have too though? What about his family? Do they want me around? Do they need me to understand that I am not family? Does my face look different? Do I look like a reject? Can people see inside me? Why are they trying to beat me down? Do they want me to hurt? Did they want me to think, I do not matter?

Am I special? Am I bad luck?

Was evil born in me? Am I cursed? Am I a bastard? Did I cry too much as a baby? Is God real? Are we aliens? Why am I a girl and not a boy? Do I have a purpose?

Do I have a reason to be here? Can I make a change? Will I matter? Will I make my voice heard? Will the people Listen? How can I make them pay attention? Will I have enough time to make my voice heard? Are all girls in America going thru this?

Do we all feel sad as teenagers? If indeed we are growing why so much judgment?

What is going on with my hormones? Do you want to help? Or do you just like to hear and gossip? Why so much hate? Where is the opposition coming from?

At the age of 16 who got me? Would anyone ever really be available? Should I beware that this is my fate? What type of game is this son? Is there

Something about my body that I should know. Is my body Special? Hmm, are women everything? Could we be God?

Are we supreme beings; us humans?

Or are we just mere peasants?

Just as dogs and cats roaming about. You want me to trust you? Really? I do not trust anyone, you heard me. I lied, I trust me, but, what about you?

You want me to be scared? How is that fair? What am I supposed to fear and at what point is it ok to not be scared? Do you have all the answers? Just because you accept something does it really make it right? Do they want me to be fake? How do you do that, is that not fraud?

Can I win at this game? Why do I think the way I do? How can I be the problem? All the time or every time?

Do parents do any wrong? So only my behavior is incorrect? Never pretended to be flawless, so why the dislike? You want me to be unsuccessful? Do you need to make sure that I never feel good enough? Well, can you imagine that? Seriously, I admit my wrong, do you? Do they see my hurt and pain? Do they think I am stupid? How do you know if you are special anyway?

Why are they after me? Why are they waiting for my downfall? Why do they look at me as if I am filth? Will I ever be welcomed anywhere? Will I ever be enough?

Are they apologizing for their actions? Are they narcissists? Am I a narcissist? Matter of fact am I delusional in this bitch?

No disrespect to you, the reader. These are just many of the questions that

Go thru the minds of teenagers, humans.

The world is so big around us. Influences are coming

From all over not just the immediate circle.

Family, friends' groups, and organizations. Hormones are rising and emotions are weird. Trying to find your place and where you belong and manage

Everything going on within. That is a daily struggle all on its own. Add all these other random factors and add 100 % more stress.

Just imagine the mind of a teen daily.

So many questions, not enough answers.

WHY BETTER YET HOW

I just did not understand how HOME, really can be or was being taken away. If my mom was my actual mom and I lived in her house. How was she able to just throw me away? Could she just have banished me from the home like a stray dog? Honestly, I did know it was coming soon enough, just not this quickly.

Most kids must worry about getting good grades. I had probably been told for at least a year that I was going to be ejected off the island. Except this was anything but a reality show. The thought of being put out of my home was all I could seem to think about. My mom was very adamant about not wanting me in the home. It was as if sometimes she could not wait for the day. Almost like a kid waits for Christmas gifts. Heavy on my mind as I attended high school, trying to mother my daughter. Everything just seemed to begin to go downhill.

My behavior reflected my being in a home that was so controlling and abusive. My mom was the dominant force in my home, and it was her way or no way. She was being ruled by her past hurts and family issues. As a young girl, my mom had endured abuse at the hands of the adults, she trusted to take care of her.

My mom had the tightest grasp on me, because of this. Who would blame her in this crazy world? But it was almost as if she did not want me to know that more or better even existed. Not wanting me to know what existed outside of the home.

Feeling as if I would yearn for more as if she were herself afraid. This behavior left me with no freedom to do anything, not even think on my own. Things were going from bad to horrible this was never going to be a situation where I was in control.

At home, I was this little chill, girl with no permission to do anything. At school, I was a little bit freer to express who I was. This is probably why I was in so much trouble at school. The dawn was fast approaching, and my fate was being sealed. What I knew as normal life would soon change forever. When I tell you, I could feel this situation happening all over me. It was as if I had seen the future and what I knew; was now coming to pass.

Nothing I was doing was accurate, or so it seemed from my mom's perspective. Now some of the crap that I was doing was a bit over the top. Like for instance, I was always fighting, but those chicks did not like me. They were always picking on me. They picked on my hair, my clothes, my shoes, the fact that I was smart/nerdy. What am I supposed to do?

What were they hating on to this day I cannot explain? I did not have anything for anyone to be jealous about. Not anything, I was skinny, and my mom dressed me funny. Who would blame them for laughing it was a very humorous situation? One day on the way to school, I took some different clothes and while walking to school I changed.

The kids at school would say, "When your mom start letting you wear stuff like this?" The kids were mean to me. Indeed, I was different, I stuck out like a sore thumb.

My mom would send me to school in dresses that looked like tablecloths. I was the center of so many jokes and laughs in school. I had cousins who went to the same school as I. We had some of the same friends and they never knew that we were family. Of course, they were related by my stepdad. So, it wasn't like blood, just dang, they didn't even want to be connected to me at school. Not sure if they wanted to fit in or were just being afraid of rejection for being related to me. Either way, they did not want people to know that we were related. Looking through the eyes of a child, you see so much going on. You never know how to fix some things or where to begin to complain. Who would listen to me if I had said anything?

Growing up we weren't wealthy more or less a middle-class family. In the neighborhoods surrounding the area I lived in, wealth was abundant. Yes, there were children whose parents were company execs but not my parents. So, I would get confused when people would mistreat me. Might have tried to understand what was going on if there were not any problems in the house. To me, it was just too much all the time very consuming. Kids will be kids and that's what children do. They see something funny and make jokes. I didn't go through this in church just at the school I attended.

Why did people act this way? What was really going on in my world, like seriously? Couldn't understand how I didn't want to judge anyone, but everyone seemed to be judging me. I would never follow suit and just treat people some way because of what others said. If this is the norm for most humans, I wanted no part in it. How superficial are those that acted this way I thought? Why were people so deceptive, misleading, and judgmental? Someday I cared some days it was just taking too much effort to care.

Stressed and in so many toxic settings I gave up, I know I gave up. For whatever reason, it just did not matter to anyone, not even me. But what if it did matter though, and mean everything in the world? Just what if? What I do know is once I left that home It was the last time, I ever felt comfortable for an exceedingly long time.

What steps I should take to get help, I hadn't a clue. So, I felt the best answer was to just prepare to go. The previous year I had just given birth to my first child at the age of 15. That was a huge situation all in itself. I got pregnant at 14 by a guy I went to school with. He and his family wanted no parts of me or my baby. I couldn't explain that either, before the baby was born, we were ok. Once he found out I was pregnant, he even stopped talking to me at school. More and more rejection coming towards me.

So much that my little self just could not seem to comprehend. What did I do so wrong to him, shucks, I let him have my body did not that count for something? Labor and delivery oh my, was I becoming a woman? My body went through more changes that year than ever. Would I be this way forever or would my body return to normal?

Once my daughter was born alive and well, I was thrilled. The delivery of my daughter was scary as hell. Didn't know how to push they ended up using forceps. They were scared she was not growing cause my body was so little. Also, the fact that I was a teenager was a big worry. My mom did not really prepare me for motherhood, she was having a hard time dealing with the fact that I was having a baby. Did not know if she was shy in the Sex area or if she just did not know how to talk to me about things. Growing up children need guidance all my mom said was do not do it. Really mom you got to give me more than that. My friends were like it was the best thing ever. Curiosity had definitely caught the cat.

There were a lot of emotions surrounding my teen pregnancy. My mom probably felt like she had failed at being a mom.

My little girl is pregnant, what must they think of me?

Mmm.... She should have let me talk to them judgmental

Opinionated men and women. You are not supposed to look down on anyone. You never know just when the tables may fuck around and turn. My mom sacrificed for us, she provided for us, she protected us to a fault, she stuck in there even when she did not know how to handle situations.

My pregnancy surprise being one of them. She was not a bad mom because I was a teen mother. I never thought that ever about my pregnancy.

We definitely had a mess on our hands. Real things happen to real people. Shucks other than the emotional abuse, control, and overprotectiveness, my mom was cool. She had moments when she laughed, I mean she would be so happy. It was as if she let her guard down and was that little girl from way back, before her abuse. When she laughed, we all laughed. Yes, I am compassionate towards my mom because I know what she has been thru. Did I think it was an excuse for her behavior?

Hell No! In no way shape form or fashion. In the back of my mind, I know she did not appear to care about me. However, I knew she was hurting, I just did not understand why I was the target of the hurt.

Why beat up and bully me. I had to be mature in certain situations, mommy never gave me credit for anything. So, since mommy could not talk to me about sex, having a baby, and those growing up issues. I settled on talking to peers, older than me and younger than me. There were not too many secrets between us kids we talked like we were big grown experienced people. All that talking still didn't prepare me for what I was to experience. I thought pushing meant one thing the doctors and nurses felt as if I was straining. After I have the baby then they tell me to push as I must poop.

Everything turned out amazingly well, regardless of what I knew and didn't. I was actually a mommy to someone, to me that was the sweetest thing on Earth.

The nurses said, "I was the youngest mom that gave birth in the maternity ward that whole week." They really catered to me and made sure I was resting. How about they knew things were about to get real when I got home. To them, I was a stranger, they were women and I mattered. Nurses are caring and have big hearts, plus they knew that newborns were a lot of work. There were some things to come that I would never have ever imagined. I do believe those women looked at it that way. Most 15-year-olds were not delivering babies, they were actually learning themselves. Finding their place in the universe we lived in. Not me! Oh, no, I was having a baby, becoming a mom caught all up in the mix.

My daughter was such a beautiful baby to me. She had the biggest little eyes; I had ever seen. They say when you pick on someone during your pregnancy your baby comes out with those issues.

I picked on my homegirl the whole time I was pregnant. She had huge, big ole eyes, my daughter had huge, little eyes. 5'lbs 6 oz. Was how much my baby girl weighed.

This beautiful bundle of joy made me feel like I had done something correctly. At least In my eyes, I was pleased with myself. A very painful experience of my body, my menstrual cramps were so painful that they prepared me. Cause other than that, nothing could be compared to the pain of giving birth.

I remember thinking that I would eventually have to take her away, my baby. These people would hurt me they would hurt her too if they got the chance. I promised her she would never suffer the hurt I did. Not so sure if I myself had gone into protection mode. Either way, I vowed to protect her with my life, they would never hurt her the way they damaged me.

If I didn't fight for anything, I would fight for her. She was of great value to me and yes, she would know. I would encourage her, love her, be there for her as a voice of reason and let her live her life in freedom. She was mine, she belonged to me and there was nothing any one of them could ever do about it.

Oh, but having a baby was full of surprises. It was definitely no walk in the park, not even a stroll. Adding to the adventure kind of makes life worth living. So, I embraced it all. So many things that I had no clue how to deal with were happening in my life. When I tell you, this baby did not like to sleep at night. America, she just wanted to be played with. She loved being talked to especially at 2:00 in the morning.

According to older people, this happened because while pregnant, babies learn their own sleeping patterns. Totally unprepared I just knew night meant to sleep for humans. How quickly I learned that was not the reality for babies, especially newborns. Her days and nights could not be more confused. Did I get a wake-up call? Indeed, I did, I was wide awake, literally, I was ready though, felt like with a little help I could do this. So positive and full of excitement, I was not alone anymore. I'm not sure why I thought having a baby would make my life better.

In my defense, I was 14,

You know what they say when I was a child, I thought like a child. This was not Barbie and her friends I learned; this was real-life lessons 101.

I knew it wasn't a make-believe circumstance. Just didn't know how real things were going to be for me. Not going to talk too much about being 14 and pregnant. That is another book I have been working on. However, it's hard to give you some history,

Without touching on being 14 and pregnant

Already looking and feeling like a statistic my destiny did not seem like a journey, anyone would want to travel. Sixteen, being kicked out of the house, I was about to now be homeless with a baby. Was I the prodigal child? I always tried to relate things to what I was being taught in church. Since that was our go-to, but that wasn't making any sense either.

The next thing my mom said was, "I know I said you can take the baby, but I changed my mind. The baby will continue to stay here with me." I couldn't take my daughter with me. Was I hearing her correctly, I could not take my daughter! What?

How is that righteously ok? So, I had this baby and because I am a teen mom, I have no rights? How the heck is that fair? How could she change her mind so fast? What happened that made her feel this was even allowed? I might not have known what I was in store for, but really. So, because I was underage it was ok for my mom to just take my child. Not even that, she had just gone to court and took custody of my child and had documents to prove it. How was that even legal in America?

Why wasn't I subpoenaed to come to court? Did the judge know

I had the baby? What was her point, what exactly was she trying to portray me to people as?

These are the things my little mind would wonder about all the time.

She explained that for my daughter to get medical help or care she had to be on her insurance.

I was like, but how is that; should not she have to be on her mom's insurance? Which I had none or maybe I did. So, confusing to be so young and must make such adult decisions. What was an adult decision anyway?

Man, what a wake-up call in the middle of the winter. Not sure to this day why my mom and I had all these problems, or why she chose to discipline this particular way. I just figured there were so many people and influences in my mom's ears. Very opinionated people. Those that she chose to seek counsel did not have a pregnant teen. They had children that were doing outstanding things probably, who knows. For the record why do people advise in situations that they do not know of? It's something I will never understand.

It's like me not knowing how to put wires in a house but trying to tell you what to do. Or speak about something that I do not know of. Somebody would pick me up for murder. Cause I had to be trying to kill some folks. You cannot give directions to places; you have never physically been.

You get my drift.

I know she was embarrassed that it happened to her family. Do not think the embarrassment would be the emotion I picked. However, it's not the 1900s either. And unfortunately, this was happening to us, especially me!

How and Why?

My answer

Life happens.

The how would be that I had sex unprotected. Why, why is such a powerful question it takes all the confusion away. Simply put, I wanted a baby. So, I engaged in sexual activity. It wasn't the end of the world, nor did it make me a bad person. Some say, well she could have been a blessing, but timing is off.

How is that an acceptable statement? If the timing was wrong then she is wrong, right? See how confusing this mess can be. A gun was not put to my head, I did not have to have sex. Unless I was married, I should not have been, but I did.

These are my consequences. Fully I was aware of this I knew 2 things would happen from having sex. Catching a disease or getting pregnant. Did not know it would happen to me, but I wanted a baby. Unfortunately, things do not always go as planned.

I was just too immature to actually understand any of this.

A LITTLE MORE BACKGROUND

So, let me just start over and give you some background. I just turned in and was on a roll. I was born in Wilmington, Delaware July 1975. The hospital that I was born in was Wilmington General Hospital. Not there anymore, I guess the city decided to condemn the building. Don't know too much about the history of my life in that state. Anything I know I was told because I was too young to remember. Everyone has so many stories of how I was born. Such a cute baby, so hairy.

Mommy said, "You were the only baby in the nursery that looked like a monkey. You had hair all over your body." She bragged because of my Native American roots. A baby born with my exceptionally large curly locks, they all seemed to agree. According to the stories I was told by my mom, family, and friends.

I and my mother went traveling after I was born. Trying to find her place in the world she decided she wanted to start traveling. She had decided to travel to Oklahoma after I was born to see my uncle and his family. Things were not going so well for her in Delaware. Now being grown, she was able to roam as she pleased. So, she started her quest by traveling out west. She went to go visit her big brother and his family.

They lived in Oklahoma City; this would be both of our first time traveling there. From Oklahoma, she went to Virginia to visit her other brother and ended up meeting the love of her life so she decided we would live there when I was 2 years old. While in Virginia my mom decided to not return to the state of Delaware. Looking to start her life's journey,

Love, at first sight, was all I ever heard about my mom and stepdad.

They kicked it right off the start and begin what they call courting. Not even sure what that has to do with dating but ok. Soon after meeting, they decided to get married and start doing the family thing.

I do remember as a child having family in Delaware and visiting Delaware. Especially during the Christmas holiday season. Waking up to a white Christmas was such a beautiful thing. Those visits were short-lived, and we were in town for maybe a day or three. These family trips were not taken to often as you can imagine. So other than my mom and siblings, my stepdad's family was who was nearby. I grew up in Chesapeake for my early years. I can at least say from kindergarten to a couple of grades later we lived in that city in some apartments.

When I was the age of 7 my mom told me that I had a Real Dad. She explained to me that another man had helped her make me. I did not really understand what she was trying to say. It did seem, however, like she was telling me I had a different dad. Like my dad was my dad, but he was my stepdad. I had another dad, but he was not around because he did not want me. Not sure what came over me, I begin to cry. She went on to say that he didn't believe I was his child and threw a dime at me for child support.

Another dad, I thought. Who was this mystery man? What did he look like? Why does he not want me? Was I going to meet him, could I meet him? What if he doesn't want to meet me? Why not want me? Did I have to meet him? Why do I have to know about him if he doesn't want me? I thought that was horrible. Like I think this was the very first scar that cut super deep almost instantly.

My little mind did not understand or comprehend what was actually going on. Especially with men, women, or relationships at the age of 7. Why was I so different? Most all my peers lived with their mom and dad. They looked

Liked these people, I knew I didn't. I could hear the whisper and conversations I walked into. Was I the only kid who had another man as a dad? Was this not normal? Did I look like him?

Why my mom chose to tell me this bit of information at that time.

I am unsure. It was hurtful to me, shucks, I thought I was an ok person. Probably would not have mattered when I was told that bit of information would have stung at any age period. My mom told me a few weeks later we were going to be traveling.

"We are about to go on a vacation to Delaware to stay at your aunt's house." She said. A few weeks later we ended up traveling up north. While we were there on vacation, I had the opportunity to meet my Real Dad. For the first time, according to my mom's story.

Think I was at my aunt's kitchen table and my mom called my name.

She was talking to a tall gentleman through my aunt's screened door. When I walked over to them, the man smiled. "Do you know who I am?" he asked. "No!" I replied. My mom stepped to the side so we could be face to face. He looked me straight in my eyes and smiled again. "You don't know who I am?" he asked again.

I laughed because he was funny whomever he was. He leaned in close to my ear and spoke. "I am your daddy," he whispered. I thought he was making another joke. So, I replied, "No you're not." He looked at me seriously and said "Ask your mom, who I am." My daddy, I thought could this really be him. The man me and mommy were talking about that day in the bathroom. I moved in a little closer to look and see if I saw a resemblance.

I felt like he had my face, dang, could this be? Hold up I was unsure so many emotions overcame me. I looked at my mom. I needed her approval to make sure these were indeed facts. Was this my dad, I asked her? She replied, "Yes."

Wow, just wow. After my mom told me about him, I wanted to meet him so badly. This was like a dream come true. Where had he been? I was so incredibly happy and so excited to meet him. He grabbed me and gave me a big hug, picking me up. He was so tall, I bet that is where I get my height from. Look at his face, this was the first time I had seen anyone that looked so much like me. Or I like them. His personality was funny like mine. My mom was more serious, and I was silly by myself. He had so many qualities like me or I him. He had some people with him. I met my Uncle that day and a cousin. At the time I had 2 little sisters, one of whom was the same age as me.

How cool was that we were not twins, but then again are we? So funny, I mean we didn't have the same moms and birthdays. Let me just keep telling this story. My dad gave us some money and me and my sisters walked to the store. While walking to the store my sister said. "My dad was trying to negotiate me going with them. So, they sent us away.

"Why you live so far away?"

"I don't know," I responded.

"Dang, you look a lot like daddy!" She said.

"I know that's so crazy, right?" I replied

"You should come live with daddy; we would have so much fun."

"You should ask your mom if you can spend the summer,

With daddy or something." She said

"I will," I replied. "My mom might say yes, I don't know though." I continued

"Do you get to see him a lot?"

"Who?" She replied

"Daddy!"

I had called him Daddy for the first time.

"Yes, he comes and gets me on the weekends sometimes."

"Why can't you just come to stay with your aunt?"

"I wished you lived here." She seemed to say all at once.

"Me too"

Really, I did, I didn't even know I had sisters. What an awesome surprise. Mommy had only told me about a dad, but that was it. Wow, this was so cool.

Was that even an option to come and live with my dad? Would my mom let me come visit daddy? Virginia was so far away. My daddy, I had my own daddy and to me, that was a special thing. People would ask my mom whose child is this she looks different. Now I knew where I belonged. I could see both my mom and dad in me. My other little sister was really small, we just babied her and carried her wherever we went. When it was time for them to go.

My dad asked my mom,

"Let me take Raylene with me for a little while please."

My mom replied, "No, I don't think that would be a good idea."

What did that mean? She didn't think me going with my dad was a good idea. Why did she allow me to meet him? Why didn't he just take me anyway? This wasn't fair. My mom didn't care what my dad said. She wasn't ready for that and well he just let her have her way. Gave me a big hug. Told me he loved me, and he would see me soon. My sister and I exchanged addresses. We decided since we were so far away, we could be pen pals or something.

We did not have too many options as I lived so extremely far away. My mom and dad did not seem to like each other, and they were so different. My mom was uptight and mean to my dad. I couldn't tell what they actually were disagreeing about. Back in those days, we weren't allowed to be in adult conversations.

I want to say that was another situation that changed my life forever. Once I found out that I had my own dad, I felt a little special. My confidence changed a little. Even though they were far, they existed, and they belonged to me and they were my family, they seemed to genuinely care, and we looked so much alike it was scary. A lot of questions I had in my head were answered through me meeting my dad that day. Think my dad wanted to see me before I went back to VA. My mom wasn't compromising her schedule and I think there were some more conflicts.

Once we left to go back to Virginia, I never saw my dad again until I was kicked out of my mom's home.

We continued to live in the same section of town up until the 3rd grade. We then moved to Portsmouth, Virginia since my mom and stepdad bought a house.

Me, my brother and sisters lived ok for the most part. However, I was the only child that had a different parent. Was I treated differently? I was! By my parents, friends, and family. Now do I think it was all done intentionally? No, maybe not, but I mean, regardless, it did happen! Yaw know life happens regardless. Life can also be quite harsh at times as well.

My mom treated me differently with little settled things. Other times I may walk upon a conversation like "That baby doesn't know she isn't his child. They need to tell her" This was coming from some of my stepdad's, random family members.

My mom might say something like you stand like your daddy or refer to a trait that I and my dad shared to help me remember I was different. Now everyone who knows me knows that I smoke Hella weed. My lips have always been dark since before I ever started smoking, they just genuinely were darker brown lips. Especially my bottom lip. I never knew it was really dark until my mom was teaching us how to apply, makeup.

My mom told my sister that this lipstick color looked so good with her it matched her skin.

I asked mommy

"What color lipstick matches my skin color?"

She replied, "I don't know, you have them dark people's lips" (inserting my father's last name into the conversation) She said "I don't know how to blend lipstick with dark lips.

What would you have me to say, I cannot make this shit up?

So yes, I was treated quite differently at times. I do not know why mommy was so mean to me, but I did feel like she hated me growing up. I would wonder what had happened between her and my dad that would have turned on me. Anyway, that was life so either I cry over it or push just a little bit more. With my mom's feeling, however, she felt it did not help for me to add my hard head to the mix.

There is not enough time in a day to worry about all these extra things. The who, what, when, where, and whys. You have to just keep pushing and that's just what I have been doing ever since. Feeling like an outcast growing up could actually have benefits. It may have not been all bad. I know how it feels to be the odd person standing out. When I see people being treated like outcasts I can relate. Well, I think it is more like a rejection.

My heart is big, and I just want everyone to be happy. I realize that may not always be the case. My story could help somebody, even if just one person. One grandmother, mom, sister, daughter, or niece. Maybe even a father when it comes to his daughter. If I help them pay more attention to their child and themselves. We might just have some healing in America and a little less suffering.

Getting over rejection takes hard work and the battle is conquered daily. You must reprogram your mind to relearn your outlook on things, just correctly this time. You have been taught, trained, mentored, or coached incorrectly. Based on some type of pattern or cycle from the teacher. They could have been incorrectly taught as well, but the cycle must stop somewhere. My mom might not have known she was in a cycle or she might have known and not cared.

Most abuse victims either over-protect or repeat cycles that they despise. Until you, heal you cannot heal or show someone else how to heal. What hurt in the past doesn't have to be in the future.

When I was in school, I was picked on because of my clothes.

Fashion was never my mom's favorite pastime. I mean she dresses me funny, kids at school targeted me, but it was not that hard to do. Please forgive me, but

This is my story I laugh a lot, especially now. Hopefully, you can too. If you saw me, you would probably laugh too. Where did she find these garments to dress me in?

People overlook people daily because of things they have no control over. So, it's true and funny at the same damn time. I wore shoes that old women would wear that were like 60. Ask me how I know.

The cafeteria lady had the same shoes as me one year in 6th grade.

I promise it caused a fight because people would pick and talk shit and well. I told my mom; these shoes are not for little girls she did not care. I'm convinced she bought them because I pointed out they were old people's shoes. She didn't care what I looked like, she enjoyed dressing me like a clown. I guess or maybe she did not care about what I endured every day as a kid. Maybe it was not important to just look though, these shoes were in the elderly section. They were therapeutic soft sole shoes.

LMAO. The kids would pick on me, I mean. I got in fights defending myself in school because I looked funny. Mostly I felt disrespected, on those grounds alone. They did not respect me because I wore dresses all the time. Then the dresses always look like a tablecloth your granny would use for Thanksgiving when the family got together.

I was very petite, like a stick, not even 100 lbs. Since I was so tiny you couldn't just put any clothes on my petite physique. Absolutely no shape at all no breast no tidy at all I got stories for days. No hips or thighs just a little innocent girl. Guys were not really paying me attention because they had reps to uphold. They could not be seen with Raylene plus there were prettier girls, girls that could dress, and girls that could talk on the phone and hang out. I was kinda-sorta in some type of prison, so none of the boys were actually paying me attention.

Look at me now! Ok, I was feeling myself a little bit. I just had to shake up the mood a bit. Teenage girls and their moms can be a hard-emotional topic. Moms and their mini-me. Probably we need to be able to freely talk to a counselor as part of premenstrual issues. Counseling is good and should not be frowned upon so often.

Hormones are a motherfucker, add sex and emotions in the mix.

All the while trying to juggle your friends and family. Woo-sah! I and my mom bumped heads a lot, but I mean in Our defense, she nor I had any rule books on how to be a mother or daughter lol. I always felt my mom was a bit manipulative, narcissistic, and controlling. These could have been learned behaviors because she had other sides. Sometimes she appeared to be so happy and cool. I believe she greatly cared about how she was seen by others.

She just was not so accepting of her own self. She was diagnosed with mental health issues that I do not understand totally. Listen, I just found out in 2008 that bipolar was a real mental health issue. I thought it was just a saying people were using. My sister would say "My bipolar acting up." Who knew this was a real diagnosis?

Mental health disorders are real, and more people suffer from them than we know. Some people don't realize their abilities and strengths. Some people just can't cope with everyday normal stresses. While others can't help anyone because their mental health is so severe. Mental illness can be caused by a ton of things, genetic factors, biochemical imbalances, environmental stressors. However, they may need proper care and treatment to learn to cope and recover. People with mental disorders should not be picked on.

When I and my siblings were kids anything, we didn't understand we laughed at. There is absolutely nothing funny about mental health illness and disorders. They should be handled with care and understanding. We all must take responsibility for our wrongs as best we can without excuse. If I am raped it is not for me to rape again, but to help protect myself and others from being raped as best I can. This is just an example of breaking the cycle and not allowing it to continue. Change behaviors that you can and accept what you cannot, get help, and grow.

My mom was an abuse survivor as well, so now as an adult, I get some things and yet still ignorant about others. It just really does not matter to me that much as an adult. I want her to heal and me and you and them. I have no desire to be a victim or be hurting for years over the same thing. Nor do I desire to have someone suffer continuously over decisions and real-life events.

Get Help!

People who offended me or hurt me did what they did and still, I rise. They are not in debt to me now or never.

To me what's done is done now let's move forward. Is it possible for us to heal? Yes, and if we heal, must we have healing rules or can we just Heal naturally? If I had of wrote this book at the age of 18 well it would not have been good probably just a one-sided emotional book of anger. Instead, you now get a mature woman telling her story with good intent.

Will someone find a way to make my intentions bad. Do we live in America?

I have no degrees in anything mentally related. Just life experiences and what they taught me. What happened to me might not have to happen to another. Others have suffered at the hands of abuse. No two people's stories are alike, there are no answers as to why life happens this way. What I know is hers hurt; led to my hurt. I do **hold** her responsible because she was an adult. If she knew she had problems she should have gotten help. Shucks, all she had to do was love me or maybe just showed me how to love myself.

Are we healing now?

Absolutely one day at a time.

HURT PEOPLE HURT

Hurt people hurt and that is factual, so yes, I experienced a lot. Whether people mean to hurt or not it happens. For every cause, there is an effect. My mom was a huge disciplinarian. One of my sisters told me that we received corporal punishment as children.

My mom was a firm believer of Mr. Do Right, the belt or the rod of correction. She did not have a problem smacking the shit out of you or backhanding whenever she felt the need. I personally just did not feel like all of this was necessary. However, the Bible said, "Spare the rod, spoil the child." What is up with people and this verse, parents feeling like if they don't beat their children then they don't love them. Come again, how are you relating spoil to love? This had to be my mom's favorite verse. I mean, to me it was a bit extreme, especially in specific situations. If my little brother did something, we all were beaten and disciplined because my mom just wanted us to understand that she was not to be fucked with. As if we already did not know. Have you ever seen her hands or calf muscles? She's a brick house!

One weekend I went to hang out with a friend, her mom and my mom were friends. Mommy had given me a curfew think I needed to be home at 7 pm this particular evening. Her mom had a couple of errands to run, which led to me getting home a little later than I was expected.

I explained to her I am going to get in trouble if I am late. She used her phone because I was adamant that I had to call my mom. She called my mom and explained to my mom that she would be a little late as she was running errands. She had the phone on speaker so I could hear the conversation. My mom was like ok that is fine, thanks for calling. I didn't believe her though; my mom didn't play when it came to rules. When I got home, I was beaten with a belt because I was late, before they had even pulled off good, she was beating me. My mom felt that I had disobeyed her rules and my behavior was defiant. As if I personally had said I'm doing my own thing and your rules do not matter.

The phone call was supposed to save me from the wrath of my mom. To help her understand that my being home late was not intentional, rather that it was out of my control. Mommy would have preferred for me to walk, run or fly home, as long as it was before curfew. I was 16 years old at the time, with a baby. My baby lay at the end of the bed crying as I pushed her away so I could lay there and get my beating. I did not want her to be hit with the belt. She was crying not understanding why I was crying. I was pleading for my mom to stop, but she did not. This was my punishment for not making it home on time, that night. Not saying that because I was a mom, I could not be disciplined, but she beat me in front of my crying baby. Mostly to tell her friends, you know, so she could have a story to tell of how I thought I was grown but she showed me.

I just wanted to know, was this the appropriate punishment. Is this the only way that I could have been taught that my mom was not playing? Even though all I was doing was coming home to sit around like I did every day, I was late, that is all that mattered to my mom. She needed to make sure that her point got across. Really America? I was already a mom myself, glad my daughter did not understand because that was humiliating.

There had been several times before that this type of treatment had been handed down from my mom. One day in 7th grade, an excessively big guy was walking down the hallway. He purposely walked past me and stepped his big foot on my shoes. I pushed him and said, "You didn't even have to step on my shoe, I wasn't even bothering your big ass." Maybe, just maybe that was what upset him, but I meant that. What reason in the world did he have to be walking so close to me in this oversized hallway, that he stepped on my toe. That had to be the best intentional accident ever.

He got close I threw up my set and well, we immediately started fighting. I told the principal "Please don't call my mom up here,"

It's not my fault. He had students who witnessed the fight, I, Raylene was not at fault. However, because I was involved in a physical altercation at school, they had to call my mom. While talking to my mom on the phone, mommy said, "What did I tell you I was going to do if I got another phone call from your school?" I pleaded my case with her. "Mommy it wasn't my fault I cried; I have witnesses." The principal asked for the phone back, he wanted to explain to my mom it was just a courtesy call, because I had been in a physical altercation it was protocol to contact a parent. Not sure what she told him, but he begins to argue with my mom on the phone.

After seeing that he could not get a word in edgewise, he said, "Yes, ma'am." He then hung up the phone. He looked at me and said, "I am so sorry, but you were right, I should not have called your mom." I said, "She is coming to get me and take me home to beat me." I explained that my mom said she was tired of coming to the school. It did not matter what happened the next time she received a call from the school she was coming with the belt.

My mom came up to the school, I saw her from the window as she parked in front of the school. When I noticed the belt around her neck I tried to run to the front door and meet her, so she didn't have to actually come into the school. Didn't want any of the other students to see my mom with the belt around her neck.

The way the school was set up the cafeteria was located by the front door and the sidewall was glass. Anyone on either side could see each other and it was lunch for 6th graders. My mom insisted that she needed to speak to the principal. She was carrying my baby sister in her car seat as she walked into the front office. All eyes were on my mom because she had a belt around her neck, they didn't know exactly what was going on, but they knew someone was in trouble. The principal took us to his office and told my mom that he felt she was being irrational about the situation. He asked. "Why did you come up to the school with a belt on her neck?

She replied. "This is my child, and I will discipline her as I see fit."

He said, "You do not have permission to beat her on school grounds, I do not approve, and I will call the authorities."

She told him to do what he saw fit and said. "Raylene Come on."

So, I followed her into the girl's bathroom that was right across from the cafeteria. Students were walking out as we were walking in. I prayed that nobody I knew was in the restroom. Mommy put my sister's car seat in the sink and said.

"Lay down."

"Mommy. Please don't do this, Where?" I asked.

"Right here." she pointed to the floor.

"Mommy, you want me to lay down on the floor right here?"

"There are people still in the bathroom," I said.

Whoever was in the bathroom stall. Their feet were showing from the bottom of the stall.

"You should have thought about that before you got in the fight." She replied

"It wasn't my fault." I pleaded with her

"Lay down!" she replied.

So, I did, and she beat me right there in the girl's restroom while my peers were present.

It was not even my fault.

All this big old dude had to do was say excuse me. He had inconsiderately stepped on my foot. All I wanted was an apology or something, but now he couldn't even say excuse me. Next thing I know we are fighting because he felt disrespected. Big ass, man, stop playing with me. I was not going to back down I was in the right.

Do you even know how embarrassing that this predicament was? She did not come prepared to hear me out at all. That was so hurtful. My own mom didn't love or care for me enough to even hear my side of the story, that was very painful. Now that is not to say I was innocent all the time.

Just how can I have a voice if no one is listening?

We could have had a simple conversation that would have ruled, belts out. During my upbringing, kids are to be seen and not heard. Which has got to be the most ridiculous crap I have ever heard in my entire life. Children are small beings who don't understand everything, but everyone has a voice. That's why so many families overlook molestation because they refuse to have an ear or use their ears and listen. All children do their share of crazy mischievous things.

These are all a part of growing up. Normal shit people.

I also did my share of extra Ray Ray bullshit, which comes with the territory. I never understood why my mom chose to do the things she did when it came to discipline.

I fought hard and long to get my mom to hear me out to the point of exhaustion. She never got the picture

That I needed her love.

I ran away for the first time at the age of 14. I was sick and tired of being mentally and emotionally abused, beat, punished for things I did not do. The home was complicated, to say the least. Being rejected and feeling defeated was a normal life. Anywhere had to be better for me than home, so I left. You should feel loved when you are home right? I felt anything but love at home.

On this one night, I chose not to come home when I was supposed to. I had tried to run a couple of times, but my parents ran after me and made me come back home. Possibly because I was trying to run away while we were in the middle of conversations. They would be talking about what punishment I was about to receive, and I would take off running. Only to be tackled to the ground.

One day I decided to skip school, my reason for skipping school were many. When at home, I wasn't allowed to go anywhere my mom wouldn't allow it. I wanted to have fun, just sick and tired of the same old merry-go-round. I was allowed to be at home, that's it. Tried to join sports so I could find a means of escape. It worked, but outside of sports, there were no other activities than the church. There was no purpose to watch television as half the shows we were forbidden to watch.

They weren't Christian-based or had subliminal messages.

After school, I wasn't allowed to go to any games or school activities. I could be in my yard, front or back. If I wanted to walk down the street, I had to have a reason. This reason may not be good enough to even get me out of the house.

I would go to school only on days when we were taking quizzes or testing. The rest of the day I'd skip. I was in a lot of accelerated classes. My grades were great, and I was hardly there. Encouragement has been just not something I was getting from anyone around me. Other than the actual teachers that saw that I learned on a higher level. You know how when people see you achieving, they give you a little push of encouragement. There was a lack in my life in the area of support, so I didn't get that push to press on.

I, my crazy self I got caught skipping school.

The school had called early, and my mom was home to take the call. Well, unfortunately, you know that I was in big trouble. My mom's fist fought me like I was one of her peers.

The first chance I could, I took off running, ran right past my stepdad, and out the door. My mom yelled for him to catch me and he did. I was chased and tackled to the ground in a neighbor's yard. I think someone should have told me that was not the correct way to run away. It was going left for me; how do you mess up running away.

Figured I had to get smarter than my parents and outsmart them. The next time I ran away I would change my hair so that I would blend in with society and my mom could not find me. The next time I ran away, I did just that. By the time she came to get me she did not even know who I was I had to call her by her first name to even get her attention. Funny to me now, but not at the time. I have healed but I promise you I did not want to go back. I lied to people who knew me just so I could stay at their home for the night. Got on the phone called random numbers so they could hear a voice on the other line and allow me to stay, they would think I was talking to my mom.

"Mom, I know I waited too late to call, I know mom."

"Can I please stay?"

Pretending to have a conversation with my mom.

"I know, but this is the closest house I could find."

"I told my mom. Just lying, but they didn't know, and I wasn't going to tell them. Look, I knew how to act I took drama in school.

I crack myself up sometimes!

Everyone who grew up with me as a little kid knew my mom did not play. In some places, my ass just was not allowed. I promise you when I ran away, I went straight to those specific places that I should not have been.

Me blending in as I call it, I play hide and seek well.

My reasoning for picking these select specific stories was just to give you a background. You know just a little history of me and my mother's toxic relationship. I figured if I gave you a little of what led to this moment, you may understand more.

I learned the ends and outs of what people expected or how to please because I didn't want to upset my mom. It went from my mom to the next person until it became a part of me. Just neglecting my needs and trying to please everyone.

What a waste of time, half of the people I was trying to please did not even give a dam. When it came to my mom, I just wanted her to be ok. If she was happy then we were happy. Living amongst people who I felt rejected me, I begin to reject myself. When you do something continuously it can become a part of you. Thus, a lot of these bad negative behaviors became a part of me. So now I'm disregarding myself rejecting me, I was appearing more and more like the enemy.

Was I becoming my own enemy?

To disregard my feelings and emotions.

Such a sad way to live.

I never felt I was good enough, so sad, but deep for me at the same time.

I continued these bad patterns and connected with similar people even in my adult life.

Cycles are something serious people, that is all I'm saying period point-blank.

The first time my mother ever told me she was going to kick me out. I attempted to kill myself. I had skipped school and got caught.

I had been giving these pills after I had my daughter for pain. They were Tylenol with codeine and well, I decided to just end it all. Kick me out and send me where exactly? I was suicidal, yeah; maybe, I don't really think so. I didn't want to hurt myself. Just did not want to be here if nobody wanted me here. Looking at myself through their eyes, I guess.

How dare I, then again, I was only 15 at the time. I was like I'm going to take more than the number of pills on the container. I took all my birth control pills with my scary ass. Figured if anything else I would not have any more babies and I was good with that. So, then I took about 4 Tylenol pills. I am silly ok, maybe I really wasn't trying to kill myself. I just needed my mom to pay attention, but it was not working.

Well, turns out I was allergic to codeine, that is how we found out.

Boy, what a way to find out.

Instead of dying, I broke out in hives.

My little sister said, "Your stupid, why would you leave

Me and your daughter here?" She just shook her head.

"We don't want to be here either with this crazy lady." She spoke.

All I know is I was itching, everywhere I could not stop itching. It was itching in my body all over my body. What the hell had I done? Nothing ever goes as planned.

Went into my mom's room to tell her I could not stop itching.

She wanted to know why I was itching. I took pills, now she really had a reason to pick with me. I had opened a whole other door now. Either way, what a great way to find out I was allergic to codeine. I ended up in the hospital, I broke out in hives.

I had been asked why I took the pills and I told them that I tried to hurt myself.

My mom told the doctor she did not want me coming home, she felt I needed to be seen by a mental health specialist. After chatting he said he felt like I was ok. He did think I was suffering from something called premenstrual anxiety. The doctor told my mom he wanted to talk to me alone.

So, we chatted for a bit and he did not recommend me to be evaluated he felt I was ok. He did not think I should go get mental health in the psyche ward, but that my mom starts me in counseling. My mom disagreed, she felt I needed to be evaluated. So, I was taken to the Psychiatric hospital to be evaluated.

I was scared out of my freaking mind.

I was the only child on the Hospital psyche floor because they had no beds in the children's section. The children had a section for them, and the adults had a section for them.

Which the doctors told my mom there was no room. She told them that she felt I would bring harm to myself or someone in the home.

Me, really ok; sure, that would be the day, they just suggested she do something more outpatient. Well, my mom being who she is quite adamant about her choice and decision.

I had written all over my arms as my mom was talking. Like man this is stupid, I do not want to be here. They wanted me to talk, but I didn't want to talk to them. Especially not with my mom in the room. She would just dominate the conversation and not allow me to say anything. Adults were going to do whatever they wanted. I mean, who was going to stop them, they were the ones in control.

The nurses, doctors, and other staff members had to keep the other patients away from me. I would not lie to you about this. Sometimes when I opened my eyes the nurse would be guiding someone out of my room. The floor that I was with those people couldn't have doors. I had no privacy at all. Not one bit. Every staff member even the doctors thought this was a bit extreme. I was a child though, and who was I to say anything. Just did not understand who she was trying to convince that I was crazy, me or her?

People are busy with their own lives too busy with their own issues to find time to help others. I needed someone to be there, anyone to be a shoulder that I could lean on. That never happened, I had to lean on myself. Who was paying attention, I promise none of the adults in my life were? It was apparent that my behavior was the effect of something bigger than we spoke about. There is no way that we can have a cause without an effect. Lord help us all; this was stressful as hell.

While in the Psych ward the nurse said Ms. Williams, you have visitors. Oh, my who could it be who was here to see me? To my surprise, it was two of my family members. They came to visit me, they were so sad, but I needed to see them. They hugged me and we cried and cried, and the nurses were sad, shucks they cried too. They felt the whole situation was ridiculous. They spoke to the staff and told me to not let my mom know they had come. I never did because I don't think she wanted me to have help. For the most part, I think she wanted me to feel alone, plus they didn't really get along. They felt my mom should be ashamed of her behavior. This was a bit extreme for a 14-year-old to be going through. After speaking with the staff, they explained to me that I was having postpartum anxiety.

The doctors had told the nurses and staff that this is what I was being diagnosed with. According to them, this was normal for any women experiencing after giving birth. I didn't even understand that I was going through postpartum depression/anxiety. Hell, I didn't even know what postpartum anxiety was. My hormones were just all over the place. Postpartum anxiety is the sister of postpartum depression, the signs associated with this are excessive worrying, racing thoughts, and feelings of dread. well because I did not know what was going on, I was acting out I guess who knows.

I spent at least 3 weeks in the psych ward because I got caught. The procedure was if I went into the children's hospital we stay there and get evaluated. After a little bit of research and watching, I learned how to get myself out of the hospital.

During the first week and a half, I probably didn't participate in group meetings. I just refused to speak out of anger, I felt I didn't owe anyone any explanations, feel how you feel about me. There was no way I was mental like my mom was trying to say I was. The reason I refused to talk was that, in my mind they had already formed their opinion of me, and I wanted them to keep that same energy.

One of the counselors pulled me to the side to discuss my case.

When being asked questions, I was just ignoring the conversation. The counselor begins to talk about why I was there and when

I'd leave. Since there was no participation or response from me the counselor came and sat beside me.

Coming out from behind her chair. She basically let me know she had reviewed my case and spoke to the doctors treating me. In her research, she learned that I indeed was not in the hospital for a mental break or meltdown.

She knew I had attempted suicide, and, in my records, they had recorded my family history. The doctor knew that my mom was diagnosed with mental health issues. She also knew that I was in my right frame of mind. Even transferring from the adult to children's hospitals my diagnosis was postpartum anxiety.

She suggested that I communicate and participate in the program. The procedure was if a child came to the mental hospital, they stayed for 2 weeks. In that 2-week time period, they would be tested in several situations. I had already been in there one week on the adult floor and a week in the children's hospital when I and the counselor spoke. She hugged me and told me to release what I was holding inside.

Reassuring me that they were not the enemy and indeed trying to help. Not so sure why I trusted her, but I had to trust someone. She told me I had one week left. The shortest time a minor had advanced the program was a week. I would be the next child to advance if I let them give me some tools to help me. The next time they had a group I talked. I told them everything that I had ever endured that hurt me. The counselors were impressed because I then begin to give back. Over the course of the next days, new children came as beds opened. A lot of the children had issues and there were some that like me was just having a hard time. When I noticed the teens that didn't want to talk like me.

I would encourage them to talk and get that mess off their chest. Use these people they want to help I would tell them and then you can get on with your life. When I finally left, I had grown. They gave me skills to cope with a parent who was narcissistic and abusive. Not diagnosing my mom with any of these issues. Just stating the facts as they happened in my world. This experience was hard I think I can feel other's pains and sometimes that pain is projected onto me, well at least that is how things felt to me.

However, I am totally grateful for the family members and hospital staff. Don't think I would have been able to make it if not for them. I can't explain how scared I was to be in that hospital with those patients. They were clearly not in their right mind, not on this planet even. These issues were deep-rooted in no way in comparison to what I had going on. They were like adult bodies with babies in their souls or toddlers. That was a very painful thing my mom did, but still, I rise. No revenge ever, only forgiveness all across the board. I'd simply just rather spread LOVE!

How did I end up here and why was this the answer? I hated it at home my mom made it so uncomfortable. I couldn't run away anymore I knew this wasn't the answer because who was going to make sure the same thing doesn't happen to my baby.

NO PURPOSE

Getting kicked out at 16 was devastating, to say the least. It was almost an emotional release, but not quite. I could probably compare it to blue balls. I guess I could have used a better example. There is no doubt in my mind that I wanted to leave.

Just didn't want to leave behind anything that belonged to me. I felt there was no hope for me or my situation in Virginia. Felt like I was being thrown away like I was trash. How did I manage to cause such a disaster? If I didn't want to be there, I dam sure didn't want any child of mine there. How would I be able to protect her from the abuse I had suffered? Didn't want her to be anywhere without me.

Crushed is not an appropriate description of how I felt inside. Completely and totally heartbroken, devastated might have been a better way to describe my feelings. Even though my mom constantly threatened me with being kicked out, I wasn't prepared. Just didn't honestly believe it was going to happen. My mom was really going to just let me go, like I had permission, after all of this mess you caused, now you want to just kick me to the curb. If I take my things you won't beat me, interesting right. I now see there was about to be an exchange. My mom controlled the situation the way she wanted to a T you better believe that. She wanted to prove that she was in control, who was going to step to her on my behalf?

How the hell could I go 4 hours away from my mini-me? In my head, I would play over things that happened to me reminding myself why I had to protect my child. Her dad wasn't in the picture, so he couldn't protect her. Why was this even an option? Who was in control of parental rights?

I am unsure if I would ever be able to help you totally understand what I was going thru mentally. My mom already controls how much time I spend with my child, how much I held her, how long she could be out of the playpen, how much I could feed her. I get it I knew that I was only 15 when I had her, I wasn't retarded, I knew way more than I was given credit for. I get that a baby gets spoiled, not saying I didn't understand those things. Just wondered how can I learn from my mistake, if I don't pay for what I did wrong?

That is like me stealing from the store and my mom going to jail.

If I steal, they going to take my little ass away not my mom. That would be my new home and where I will learn my lesson. If I get a sexually transmitted disease will I or my mom take the medicine? So, if I get pregnant and have a baby who should be responsible for that baby? Me or my mom?

That is just the way I saw the situation, everyone is entitled to their opinion, this was my life, my reality.

Nothing would have ever prepared me to have a child. I was lost, those are just the facts. A kid having a kid, yep, another statistic. Throw me up on a

Billboard, so every teen in America knows who not, to follow.

However, I was willing to be responsible for my bad behavior. Whatever I had to be responsible for I wanted to handle it, I wanted all the responsibility. Everyone was telling me life is about to get complicated because I was acting like an adult. Or the fact that I had made an adult decision. Never having to deal with this situation before I didn't know what to expect.

I know that I was going to have a lot to deal with now, being a mom. Didn't know what was to come, willing to pay for all my mistakes the best that I possibly could. In my kiddie mind, I felt like I was finally going to have something for me that was mine. The way I was raised was if I messed up, I had to deal with the consequences. Taking responsibility for my issues. Guess it didn't mean this situation because I was trying to do my best. My best wasn't good enough for her.

For whatever reason, she had to control everything around me.

Not one person around me knew how sad I was. I faked everything all the time. I had to, to survive. I learned at an early age that my feelings did not matter. What I cared about and what I thought was important did not matter at all. My feelings were discarded and not taken into consideration, I was to shut up be quiet and listen. My opinion was just that, my opinion. How I felt really did not make a difference, I was not important enough for anyone to stop and see what was really going on. I had a couple of people adults maybe like one that I could actually talk to. That was it!

During these times I never understood why it seemed people were competing with me. If Raylene was a nobody I really couldn't understand why people were even comparing themselves to me. According to the way the temperature around me appeared, I wasn't shit. I didn't know that my mom had issues that were causing her to be this person. I was only 16 well that's not true, shit 8,9,10,11,12,13,14,15,16 to be exact.

Do I even get to understand that mommy, the person taking care of me was not mentally stable at times? She needed help, one time it appeared she was getting help, but I guess that is not the case. Did my dad even know her, did she know him? Outside of making me that is. I still to this day don't understand all of her issues. I never judged her for her issues as she judged me.

I just knew whatever was going on in her mind if I vanished life would be better. The things one must endure in silence, with no outlets.

NOWHERE to run to! NO ram in the bush or was this really my ram in the bush to be getting kicked out?

I loved her though. So, does that mean I loved my abuser?

Deep huh, well whatever, I just know my abuser was my mom. No books were talking about what to do when *mom is the one hurting you for teens.* I was attached to my abuser, I cared for her and her well-being. Honestly, I was upset with the people who raised her., they allowed her to be mistreated and didn't protect her thus I have no one to protect me.

I just wanted her to be happy,

what could I do to make her smile? Yeah, it is a people-pleasing spirit, so I've heard. I may have been a little codependent because of this upbringing. I do know in my adult life I was attracted to men with the same controlling and abuse tendencies as my mom. Why? You might ask would I want to be in relationships with guys who portray these behaviors? I'll touch on this in another book. The short answer is because it felt comfortable and familiar.

What does it mean to be in love with the person abusing you?

Could I have what is called Stockholm syndrome? I loved my mom and even though she hurt me continuously her life mattered to me. I knew what she had done to me, but I still loved her. I don't know why but she mattered still to me. As a child, I was trying to use emotional bonding with my mom as a survival strategy.

It just didn't work.

She knew I cared about her life and history. I was sympathetic to her situation she just wasn't sympathetic to *mine*.

Regardless of what syndrome it could be, I just needed to learn to love myself. To get to the point that I felt I mattered again. Cause I was slipping falling hard as hell.

Learning to hide my deep feelings and emotions had become the norm. I had no clue I was being emotionally abused by my mom as well. I did not know the signs of abuse and I didn't have time to research. If I had I guess some things would have been apparent. My mom was very moody and criticized everything I did.

She always dismissed my feelings and never explained hers. She was physically present but emotionally not present at all. I have always blamed myself for everyone's behavior when it came to me.

Whatever happened as a result of the relationships I found myself in.

Everything, I felt it was my fault. At this point, I am not even talking about relationships that I had romantic involvements with. It was anything period I had any involvement in.

My real self wasn't allowed to be present; she was going to be ignored anyway. Instead, she insisted on doing what would make them happy so, I wouldn't have to face the punishment. Discipline was the biggest thing I remember about my childhood.

Consequences for one's actions were most definitely always a given. To this day I am a firm believer of what is done in the dark will always come to the light. Why, because whether right or wrong good or bad there will always be repercussions.

I was tired of being hurt it was as if I gave in or sold my soul. Like my players' card was revoked before I could even get to start the game. They took all the fight out of me and I just did not want to fight anymore.

Another thing that many people do not know about me I have never actually felt safe. In no scenario or environment do I feel safe. I have suffered from much anxiety myself trying to get to a place of safety. I went thru verbal abuse as well by my mom she criticized everything I touched. She humiliated me in front of her friends, my friends whom every might watch the show. I was ignored and rejected my whole childhood.

Yes, I guess you can say I did feel like my whole existence was a fluke. I just wanted to be healthy and normal. Was it too much to expect love and receive it? What I was actually learning was what I should not have in my life. I was not aware that the behaviors I was enduring were what I was supposed to be running from.

The major reason that you should never judge a book by its cover!

There was no love and support for me, and I blamed myself for that. Every behavior that was projected onto me I blamed myself for.

I knew that I did not control my life or existence. Who else was going to take the blame for all these problems? The church was so confusing could not figure out if God was allowing it or if he just really wasn't in control my mom was. Adults were so judgmental; I think it comes from the fact that they work so much they have not really any time to think about what is being said and rationalize it in their heads. None of that even mattered, I could tell by the expressions on their faces how they felt when it came to me, all the fingers seemed to point at me. I have been trying to make it right ever since, not knowing that it is not my problem to fix!

To be honest I could have had suffered from many different syndromes. There are syndromes for every problem people face in life. Sometimes I must stop reading because I am blown away by how many different scenarios there are. While I was learning about Stockholm syndrome, I learned about a couple of other related syndromes.

Like for instance Lima syndrome, a psychological response when an abuser develops a positive bond with a victim, and they become empathetic to their circumstances. Then there was Helsinki syndrome in which a person being held captive begins to identify with and grow sympathetic to his or her captors.

Seems like a bit much but when you get to the root of things you would be surprised what exists that you never knew. I am not saying I suffer from any of these syndromes. When I begin to try to understand my issues these were just interesting finds.

The terminology gets deeper and deeper the more you research and begin to learn. Whatever my issues were I wanted to know firsthand. That way I could work on myself and make sure that I did not become the abuser. I never wanted to do any of the bad things done to me to anyone. Sounds easy but victims can turn into abusers really quick if they are not careful!

TOXIC SITUATIONS

My environment was toxic and normally I called it home. Every day was the same, not even rehearsed just the same things all the time. The church is where I spent most of my time. Listen the crazy thing about church was I could sing. Singing in the black community was popular in the talent category, Talents are taken seriously, and people take notice when you have talent. At school, nobody knew I could sing but at church, I was that chick. My God dad was the Pastor of the church the Bishop genuinely loved me. He made me sing every Sunday he could, he sang me out. That is so funny.

He was genuine but that for whatever reason, my talent, caused hate and suspicion. The grown men oh, my, very inquisitive about one little miss singer. I was not starting to develop as they say now, was I? I had not noticed but they reminded me every single time they saw me.

Fathers and Mothers pay attention to your little girls everywhere. Well, let me rephrase that. *Fathers and Mothers pay attention to your Children!*

Not just little girls but little boys too. Please protect the innocence of children. My mom's favorite place in the world was the church. The church is where a lot of mistreatment was done to me also. Church members molested me, fondled me, and put me in extremely uncomfortable situations. I tried to tell my mom. She genuinely loved these folks they could do no wrong, she was not listening.

From that point, I just kept it to myself. People would manipulate my mom and get her to let her guard down just so they could harass me. I was at least 7 the first time I was fondled at church. Around certain men, it became the norm for them to touch me. Grabbing my breast, hugging too deep, kissing me in my mouth. It was uncomfortable to have these huge fingers aggressively rubbing my vagina. I never asked for this type of behavior, it was not something that I enjoyed, or it wouldn't even be a subject. Youth leaders at the church were trying to fuck me. During this time, I was 13,14, and 15.

Full-out intercourse is what they wanted from me. They told stories about how they fantasized about me singing in front of everyone. Ask all the boys who went to school with me, I had no shape. It could not have been my body unless they were just child predators. One minister put me in some very compromising positions at the age of 12,13 and 14. It is not even the fact that I was a virgin and scared, were there no adult women giving out the sex? They were not about to put their huge body parts in my little body. That looked like it was going to hurt.

These people would come near my school I walked home they would put themselves in my direct path. Thinking I guess that there would be an opportunity for them. There were times I was cornered and told to stop being scared to embrace womanhood. Yep, right in bible study, watching me walk to the restroom. This one youth leader was having sex with another one of the girls in church. Her mom was just as trusting as mine, never saw it coming. To this day I do not even know if her mom ever found out.

She was in love with him, they had sex multiple times. On her bedroom wall, she had lines marked for every time they had sex. I remember telling her one time that he was trying to have sex with me. She asked if I was going to be scared, he wanted her to talk to me. My response was that I was scared, she said "Don't be he will be careful with you."

How are yaw having so much sex I asked, but she was raised in a single-family home. Her mom worked often, and he knew these things, he just manipulated the situation. It got to the point I could not even enjoy church; I was tired of being there and being harassed all the time. They have never seen this man as a problem, and he took my friend's virginity. He preyed on us young developing girls, always telling us God knew he had a problem. My mom would go visit friends of church members and leave us in the car.

She did not want us in everyone's house, and it was ok with us. Until this particular teen felt he could use that to his advantage. He would see my mom pull up as he looked out the window of his house run out give her a huge hug and come to the car put his hand in the window and touch my vagina. I knew it was a problem when another child was around and asked if I was ever touched by him. When we would talk about it, she said, "It hurts." I told her "He is not going to stop. If we just let him touch us, it would be over fast;" How quickly I became a victim of my society.

All he wanted to do was touch our vaginas and put his fingers inside. Once, I told him he was hurting me, and he told me it was supposed to hurt. Then told me he would be a little softer next time as if I was anticipating next time, such a perv. Every encounter together was always an opportunity to touch my body. Big pressure not like little flirts.

Feel how you want but it is

probably happening to several girls as write this now. Maybe we should be thanking God for COVID-19, giving humans the needed space. Parents all mad cause they got their children all day, who thinks like that. At least they are safe. Or are they? This was not something, I began to expect every time I went to church. Churches especially black churches allow this behavior and brush a lot of incidents under the rug. Just couldn't understand how they had all that holy spirit in them and couldn't see all the demons hanging around.

Looking at me as if I was full of negativity and its demons in the pulpit. God was showing them everything except for the things they needed to see. Predators were everywhere not just the pulpit, on the usher board even the musicians were at fault. People grownups in authority, whose care we were left in, the very people we looked up to. Just that They are highly respected adults, they were the last people anyone would expect.

They blended in well, you would choose everyone else except them because they walked with God. You look at addicts, drunks, and hoes and figure keep your kids away from them. No, keep your kids away from the ones all dressed up pretty and handsome and dotting all their I's. When I tell you, I did not have a village! I did not have a Village.

Everyone so it appeared, was working against me especially those closest. As a young girl, I was so mature. Maybe not in every facet of my life, however, I dealt with big issues. Learning intrigued me; my mind was taking pictures. Snapshots of things happening daily, weekly during the years. Storing them in my own floppy disk to playback when necessary. Understanding had not yet come, so emotions were everywhere.

Why do I have to fight so hard for Love? Why doesn't anyone care what happens to me? Why do I have to show up to get something that should just be given? Love in some dictionaries says an intense feeling of deep affection.

Raylene had that connection with no one. I had tried to speak to mom over and repeatedly. She never listened; she never valued my opinion at all. It was as if I was just put-on earth to do what she said, and I didn't think that was fair.

I had close friends that went to school in Va. they thought I should call child protective. To me that was deceitful so I would rather try harder to prove that I was worthy. That just didn't seem to work either, nothing was good enough. Unless it was about a dream or the attention, I got from singing in church.

They loved me singing. I led a lot of songs in the choir, to this day there is nothing like a good choir. I had some amazing friends and youth leaders in the church. Shout out to anyone who was there the day I fought at the church skating ring trip.

My god dad did not even trip. Our youth group finally got the chance to go to the skating rink and the whole church group got kicked out. Wouldn't you know that I was the culprit? My god dad did not care though he was easy, fasho. When it came to dreams that I had or have when I rest. My mom felt as if I was given a gift to see things in my dreams. Things may be like warnings and vision in my dreams.

Like I overheard her tell one of her church friends that she was waiting for me to let her know what she was having. She told her friends that I had not told her of any dreams recently with babies, she had many people telling her what they felt she was going to have. However, she felt if I dreamed it well there was a great possibility for it to happen. She would ask they would always be little girls. Then my baby sister came funny stuff, so I thought.

She felt I had a connection with dreams or something, I don't know. So, when my dreams failed to show the future, I figured it was all lost. No talent no purpose no reason to exist, yet still here. At school I never wanted anyone to know how hard home life was. So, I acted as if I was up on the latest trends. My clothes might have shown one thing, but I tuned in enough to try to fit in. There too I stuck out like a sore thumb. Somedays people would give my mom clothes for us and she would go through them and allow us to pick what we wanted.

Occasionally, there was an outfit that made a couple of girls at school say I looked cute. Gee whiz it took so much though, to please these dang people. People pleasing and acceptance, whoa so happy to be healing.

I learned all the secular music as they call it, I had to in this era I grew up in at random times somebody in class might just bust out rapping a song by

Tribe or the Jungle Bros and we all chime in.

I couldn't be a failure at everything, there has got to be a light somewhere.

All this mess just trying to fit in with the normal kids. My mom was tired of me. I would agree after so much toxicity we both were tired and yes maybe I probably did have a bad attitude. Whatever people, fighting was definitely a defense mechanism for me. Is it fair to say I became a product of my environment? Such a pretty face with so much going on never knew exactly where to direct all my anger.

I remember going to Waters Elementary and the counselor used to try to get me to open up. "Talk to me" she would say. I always replied, "I can't." She was like "why are you always on edge?" Who knows why, but she saw that shit. Like I said there weren't too many people paying attention. At the rate, the world is going parents be having their own issues that they must overcome.

When you add children to the mix of toxic situations, and you come out with babies like me. Everybody has a story of some kind where things just might have seemed off. We are blessed to not all be drug addict's society is a motherfucker. Toxic parents bring up toxic children who unless they chose to heal will be toxic adults.

Cycles just continue to repeat over again. Have you ever said to yourself I will never do this or that when I'm a parent? I know I said it all the time. the problem with that is sometimes we don't know when we have picked up these toxic traits. They are learned, behaviors so that's what makes them kind of tricky. All parents make mistakes like I said we have no parental compass. Parental abuse on any level is wrong.

I read once that Most toxic parents had toxic parents before them. Sometimes this can lead to a toxic family system going from generation to generation. Which could be known as generational curses. This is the reason I wanted to heal. I didn't want to pass down anything toxic. No toxic behaviors, attitudes, or relationships ever. The only way to not be toxic is to Heal. Abuse comes in all forms and sometimes is not easy to notice. Once you know what you're dealing with find a solution and Heal. ***People with eyes miss important visuals every day.***

SADDER

Just talk Raylene she would say, I know she wanted to help. Felt like I did not have time to focus on myself just no time at all to breathe. Never did I talk to that lady ever, I felt that was weak to talk to a random stranger about what was going on at home. Where I got that false information from who knows, as far as I knew she was OPP's. Plus, my mom forbids us to talk about anything outside of the home. Now I got to pack all my things and leave all my friends and my child.

I figured my mom wanted to be able to say things like. My daughter is a no-good mom. Raylene is leaving and that means I have to be responsible for this baby. Might have sounded good or made people like my mom better, who knows honestly, and who cares? Maybe made her seem like the amazing number one parent in the world. Nah, I do not agree I do not know why but I felt like my character was being attacked I didn't have any answers, I really wish I did. I feel if you do not allow a person to try you can't say that they didn't try.

Right?

The reason I say that is because my mom never allowed me to be a mom to my daughter and mess up. The opportunity never presented itself for me to be a mom. My mom decided that she was the mom to me I guess so she was the mom to my baby too. I am the one who just did not agree, I felt like let me mess up at being a mother before you tell people that I'm no good. That is exactly how I felt.

A baby I was and a baby I had just given birth to but a mom I was not allowed to be. I respect my mom for making sure my daughters' needs were met and for wanting to be a part of my daughters' village. Almost like she hadn't done right by me so she would make it up by doing extremely more for my child. It was like me and my daughter were sisters. This was weird but my mom just did not allow me to mother my child. When I tried to hold her, she would say don't pick her up she is fine. So, this is not helping me be responsible for my actions. What I am thankful for regardless of what went down is that I had a mom and that my mom was present.

I am not a dead-beat mom, instead right here ready and willing. My mom was so secretive about things though as if she were trying to deceive me. Let me give you an example. My mom said Raylene you want to go to court with me today? I must go for some things dealing with T (my daughter), you don't have to go. Me a teen laying in the bed when she said that I was like, " NO I don't want to go, do I have to?" "No, you don't have to go." She said instead of saying to me yes you need to be there I have asked the courts for sole custody of your daughter. She presented the story as if she had to go to court. If it was about my daughter, why had the judge not requested my attendance? I feel that if I had to handle the situation, with my kids. I would not have given my child a choice, rather said "Come on we have court today." Instead of giving my child the option to go to court. I would let her know that we needed to go to court and handle some serious business concerning the baby. If I was trying to gain custody of their child, I would say just that to them.

Yes, depends on so many variables. However, there is a difference in me thinking I have a choice. Or knowing that it was my responsibility to be present I bet there are older or younger people like duh, common sense. It was not common sense for me because I didn't know anything about the court and she never said she just asked if I wanted to go with her to court.

It was my moms' job since she was the controlling force to let me know what was going and why? Not be deceitful and do things behind my back and act as if I was doing wrong when I was just naïve.

Was my mom a Role model? Absolutely, all moms are and this happens with just being a mom. Is that fair shucks, not my rules?

Just how life is I am guessing. Google said the findings indicated that good teachers are enthusiastic, friendly, easy-going, and able to develop a rapport with learners.

Committed to the growth of their students, approachable, interested in learners as people, and always conscious of their status. Whatever skills I did not know as my mom and role model I believe it was her job to teach me.

Now I can say if she herself does not know what to teach well no she can't teach me. It can be very controversial to speak about. What I am saying is I was a teenager; I was not mature in anything. We were just really taking off in this body of mine.

My mother never told me the night before I needed to go to court, we have a meeting with the judge to give me custody of your daughter so I can get some things done for you, nope nothing at all. Nothing was mentioned about court until that morning. I always wonder if that's how my mom got custody of my kid. Later in my life, she tried to use that tactic to get custody of another one of my children.

We fought in court I appealed the judge's decision at the age of 18. That story is a little later just referencing the reason I feel it was done with intent. Just horrible advice if it was given by someone, if this is just her own decision, then why?

This was now my reality my mom did not allow me the option to be the mom. She just took things in her mind the way she chose and well I suffered from her decision-making process. Hell, we all suffered, the whole house was never the same. Sadder than sad was the mood, grey clouds everywhere. Depression set in like a mother fucker. Listen I cried and cried and cried some more. If that is not depression what the heck is.

I smiled though and engulfed myself in whatever I could. Music, singing, writing. My writing is weird, I can write better under stressful situations. Unless the stressful situations are what brought out the talent in the first place. Poetry I had been writing for a while. Won a contest when one of my teachers entered my poem into a magazine. She told me I came in second place; she was so excited. Her student had been in whatever magazine she entered it in and won. I saw my name in the magazine for winning. That poem was written right after I had attempted to run away and ended up back in my room. An emotional writer is what I think I am if that is such a thing.

I am in no way trying to play on your emotions. Over here I just deal with real life and real situations and this well this really was my reality. My life no actors, no scripts, no substitutes. Who would I have to impress anyway? As an adult who actually grew up, people's opinions do not matter so much anymore. Especially to how I see myself and the world. Why would I just write a whole book to get sympathy from Americans we the meanest mother fuckers alive. Hilarious, now would I try to help heal you, folks?

That might be a better solution.

We all have different traits, quality or characteristics that can help another. You know each one teaches one. Just one person that is all I need to help, one life. One mother or father, daughter, and son's relationship healed because of this story. My story, my growth, my life could fix just one relationship. It was all worth it. Positive vibes and conversations about building, saving, investing, and growing. Those are definitely my favorite ones I love. Living your best life ever. This book took a long freaking time. A lot of sleepless nights up writing and remembering how things were.

You would never know or guessed by looking at me what was happening in my everyday life. As much as I am social, I am kind of quiet at times and a loner. Be in my head, I think a lot. I always felt my life lessons were going to be able to help others somehow. So sad I found myself this free spirit, loveable brown skin girl.

My life is real my feelings are real, you can imagine what was going on in my head. At this moment felt like I had tapped out. Period! Look this indeed was an emotional situation so you may feel me, you may not. I hated myself during this phase of my life I felt like it was all my fault back then, but how?

Why was she so mean to me? I understood she hated my dad, but I felt like I was innocent. A baby, a child is what I was. For what reason would you hate your own baby? Your own little girl, your preteen and teenager. What about my presence was such a problem that you could not be in it? Why be mean to me? I mean am I not a part of her? Isn't that a part of you in there somewhere? Why not just put me up for adoption when I was an infant I would never know unless someone told me.

Is this may be a form of self-hate? Who knows but it dams sure did not feel good? I was supposed to go stay with my aunt and take my child at first. Those plans got canceled soon as I packed all my things. My aunt was way too excited, and she called every day and made plans for what we would do with me once I got there, as she always wanted a daughter and never had one. My mom did not like that, not so sure what exactly turned her off by it, but she was. She would be like who are you on the phone with, I would tell her. She never told me why or what was so bad about Delaware.

Or what actually happened in her childhood that was so bad. What was her fear, why so much anger, bitterness, and sadness? She hated that place it was too much going, and she did not have time to be on edge added to a more complicated life. Cannot say I blame her cause the city does be lit. At any time, anything can happen, and you find yourself expecting it. It's anticipated to happen eventually. With so many people and so many other factors at play. But if it was so bad, why the heck was I going in the first place?

Can someone please answer this million-dollar question? Shucks, my world took a hit I was most def going through a storm.

Now I just had to go stay with my dad. That was bittersweet I did not know him I had only met him when I was 7.

Oh wow, how quickly I forget. I saw him another time after giving birth to my daughter. We were visiting family in Delaware at my aunt's house. Cannot actually recall if it was a funeral or just summer vacation. While on the trip with my family my aunts begin to talk about my dad. Asking when I had spoken with him last and wondering why he was not a part of my life.

At this point, I did not think I would ever see my dad. It had been years he had to have forgotten about me.

They would know all kinds of information like if I had more brothers or sisters. They knew cousins that I did not that were related to my dad. One of my aunts decided to call my dad as it would anger my mom. They seemed to always be beefing about one thing or another. Between my mom and her sisters there appeared to be toxic everything, communication, relationships, and past life stories.

They sometimes all seemed to be fighting for attention or praise. Showing signs of jealousy and rage all along adding a bit of revenge. Me and my cousins were close well as close as we could be living so far apart. We just enjoyed each other's company when we had the opportunity to be together. This did not happen much with me as they all lived close, and I was a couple of hours away.

I and my cousins genuinely did not want to be like them we were young and very attentive. I am quite sure our experiences growing up were different but not too much.

We shared some of the same issues growing up being children of sisters. There was a lot of abuse they each encountered at the hands of the adults in charge. Did they get the help they needed was all I was concerned about? To me, that was all that ever mattered. Do you want to complain and look down on others?

Or do you want to actually heal from your wounds and grow?

Every meet up seemed to be more toxic than the last. For the most part, it was all of them. NO, I do not think they all suffer from the same issues. However, they are not that much different simply different levels. Probably depending on the different levels of abuse. Children are the understanding of the parental situation. You know a reflection of what they see.

If you ask me, they are never satisfied kind of people. Anyway, this particular aunt called my dad, let him know I was in town and that his grandchild was there. She did not know what he had going on, but he needed to skip on over there. If not, he would have another missed opportunity.

She assured him that they would keep my mom occupied so I could at least get to say hi. I did not know about this but the idea of seeing my dad was one I don't think I could pass up. I longed for my dad and if they could make it happen then what are we waiting for?

My aunt told me to get my daughter and walk to the corner that my dad was there, so I did. I was excited I randomly had a chance to speak to my dad. Everything I did when it came to him, I had to sneak, I was not allowed to contact him in any way according to my mom.

So, I seized every moment or opportunity that came my way.

There was a time when my mom went to visit her friend, I overheard them talking. Her friend was like, "What are you doing out here?

Oh, you must have come to let Raylene visit her grandparents." My mom said, "What you mean her grandparents I don't talk to them, people."

So, her girlfriend kind of looked at me and was like "There my neighbors, they live in the building next door on the bottom floor. She and my mom were preparing to go to the store. I did not want to go I wanted to see if I could catch my grandparents at home. Before they left my mommies girlfriend told me to go over there and meet my grandparents.

She let me know she and my mom had to travel a bit to get to the store and to take my time. She pointed out the building for me to go to and then walked into the other room.

When she and my mom went to the store. I went to the building across the way, I knocked on every door until my grandma opened the door. She knew who I was to my surprise and she said, "I knew you would eventually sneak over here to see me whenever the opportunity presented itself."

She mentioned that she and my mom's friend had discussed that I was unable to see my dad's family. They both felt it was not the correct way to handle the situation.

However, my mom her rules and that is just the way it went. My grandma was an extremely sweet lady smoking on her cigarettes as I looked at all the pictures of family on her walls. She talked to me for a while about as much as we could in the allotted time.

Before long she gave me, a hug and told me to get back next door before my mom returned. While visiting I told her I need a way to contact my dad. She gave me her number and my dad's number and all the numbers she had ever had for him. So, I had ways to contact my dad which I did when my mom was at work. That way I was not monitored. He would sometimes be accessible and others not so much.

That day at my aunts' house was the first time that someone was actually able to get a hold of my dad and get him to where I was before it was actually too late. While walking to meet my dad, my other aunts were in the house, they all were keeping my mom occupied so she did not know I was meeting my daddy.

I then walked to the corner and daddy was there. He grabbed my daughter right out of my arms. He was in love just playing with her loving on her.

He eventually hugged me and noticed I was there. Just joking he was so happy, so much time had passed I had got taller since he had seen me at 7. Well, that was short-lived, think it was not. I am unaware of what actually went down in that house that day, someone I heard was arguing with another and then it was told.

How you do not know your daughter on the corner with her dad right now. Like I told you, I myself was not there to hear what was actually said. I just know I saw my mom walking to me like Oprah on the Color Purple. As my mom was walking down the sidewalk my daddy said, 'Here comes your mom." I was like "Mannnnnnn I'm going to be in trouble".

She walked right up snatched my daughter out of his arms and told me "Let's go." I did not have any business talking to any strangers, she stated. My dad was like, "Really you going to be like that." She never looked back or responded to his comments. This was devastating. Why would my aunts call my dad to tell him I was here?

Then tell my mom before I could enjoy him and allow this to happen. What was the purpose to hurt me to hurt him? What exactly did make sense about that situation I can't tell you. I could look my daddy in the eyes again and that meant the world to me.

While I was walking to my aunt's crying his car was beside me. Driving slow as to keep up with my steps. He was like" I love you" I said, "I love you too."

He told me it was going to be ok "Don't be sad". Oh, I got in so much trouble my aunts, man They set me up! Look I would get cramps writing to you about

these women, but they might resurface in the back of this book somewhere. Here it is I am 15 and I was forced to go and live with someone that she told me never wanted anything to do with me. As true as that could be, keeping it real.

Parents don't tell your children things like that. Keeping it real you say. As adults' children don't even understand what reality is, they are actually trying to get to your level of knowledge.

As a child growing up, I had nobody pulling me close to teach.

Basically, I learned thru much trial and error. I did not have love from a grandma or grandfather that I could vent to. No one was too close to me. I couldn't be but so close to my mom's mother she hated her mom. I thought she was funny; she said all kinds of funny things. Not like my mom at all, she was not quite as reserved. More loud and bold, this is what I am thinking so let's just talk about it like Now.

She was a well know burlesque dancer in her young years. Pretty Portuguese and Native American Indian Lady. Not sure all the facts as my cousin have them all written down somewhere or stored in her brain. I was told my great-grandma was born on an Indian Reservation which is so very cool. My great grandfather was from Portugal, I had the opportunity to meet my moms' mother but not my mom's dad he had passed on before I was born, while my mom was a child. I knew he was an Indian man and a hard worker. My dad, I didn't know his parents too well you know I had to come in and play catch up quickly.

Which was so weird because they never acted like I missed a beat. They included me in conversations as if that was normally how they discussed things. As if they were there all the time waiting patiently for my arrival. My stepdad's parents had divorced, which meant we didn't get too much of my grandfather as he moved out and moved on. My grandmother continued to stay at the family home. My grandmother was extremely sweet and opinionated. There was no way I would talk to her about the problems that I was having. She was very loud not a bad thing, caused I loved her, just didn't want the whole city to like to know all my business.

I know kids in Va. always wondered what happened to me because it was weird, I had just disappeared. Did not know that cycles were already being created. It was oblivious from the scars that were being created in my life. I had sex because I longed for intimacy.

Friends probably were not the best people to be listening to. They were who I communicated with about sex cause well, they were talking. Kids at school, church events, were the only ones talking for real, we were curious beings very inquisitive. Sex however was not the reason or start of my problems just numbed the pain or so it seemed. The closer it got to the day I was to leave the more depressed I got.

I was going to meet my dad and live with him where I could talk to him and hear his side of things. This was something, that I wanted. Would also mean a lot to me as I never understood the problem. However, I could not take my daughter such a bummer.

SACRIFICIAL LAMB

When I got to the city my dad met me at the greyhound bus station. He looked a lot like me, I was not used to being around anyone that looked that much like me. He smiled like me, laughed like me and he had my face. Others would agree it was the other way around and I looked like him and laughed like him and had his face.

He smiled and gave me a huge hug; he was indeed happy I had arrived and safe. My aunt was also with my dad she knew I was coming in town and I believe she wanted to show support from my mom's side of the family. They were strangers as my dad and his family, so it was a nice gesture if anything. Daddy was so excited to take me around to meet his brothers and really anyone who knew him.

Wilmington, Delaware was remarkably interesting, after all this was the place that I actually came from. I knew there had to be some answers to a lot of my questions in this place. The day I got to Delaware while daddy was helping me get settled in, I received a phone call from my mom. She called me because she said she was being investigated for kicking me out of the home. Before I had left Va. I was in a Teenage parenting group. A group of girls from the age of 14-18. I told the people at the teenage mom group that my mom, had kicked me out. We were a group of teen girls that had babies out of wedlock and were given resources to help them continue with their education.

I was not supposed to tell anyone that my mom had put me out and was not allowing me to take my daughter but since I knew I was not coming back I did. I and the lady in charge were close, she kind of took me under her wing. She seemed really interested in what made me happy, sad, or what was really going on at home. I knew she was interested and since I was leaving why not answer her suspicion. She didn't want me to leave though I was an asset to the company, encouraging other girls to push on. The lady in charge of the group called child services on my mom and told them she had put me out or me and a baby. Not so sure what or how that actually went down.

My mom told me that she needed my help. She asked my dad to let me come down and testify on her behalf and that I would be able to get my daughter and bring her back. Omg, I thought there is hope, I can do this now my baby was coming. I would have done anything in the world shit. Trust, I would have sold my young soul to the devil. Daddy agreed that it would be ok if I were getting something in return. Not sure if he was ready to help me with my daughter, he did make a couple of calls the next two days to make sure that I had childcare.

As anxious as I was to get to VA. you would have thought a million dollars were waiting for me. I am going to jump around a bit here in the story and fast forward to this specific situation.

Then I'll go back to the event of me arriving in Delaware. The next day my dad got me a ticket and two days later I was off

to get my baby. When I arrived in Va. my mom came to the bus station by herself without my daughter. She began to explain that child services were trying to take my child and my brother and sisters. I asked why they would do that?

According to the authorities she said, "Because I had told the teen parenting lady that she kicked me out they reported her." So, I was like "I mean I understand but what does that have to do with me." She said, "I need you to let the people know that she had not indeed kicked me out but that me and my dad had chosen this."

As if I and my dad came up with the idea and she just went along for peace's sake. I never imagined that my mom would tell me to lie. Although I knew parents who did this regularly my mom wasn't one of them. I just looked at my mom this lady who hated my very existence as a child she would beat me for not standing straight wanted me to lie for her. I knew she didn't like me once moving to Delaware I was in the company and presence of people that liked me so I could see right through my mom and her sob story. I didn't see her the same anymore, I saw my mom vastly different. I asked her,

"So, you just want me to lie to these people and tell them that you did not kick me out."

She cried and said "Yes." It was the only way for her to not lose my siblings. So, I said, "I can have my daughter and take her with me back to Delaware?"

She said, "Yes, I promise I really need your help."

I do have to admit that I hated seeing my mom look like she was about to lose it all mentally. She appeared to not have the solution to fix this problem other than using me. It had to be important she had me come from Delaware all the way to VA like she had a subpoena.

We went to someplace like where you get food stamps, and I was taken in a room.

I saw the lady from the teen parenting program also in the lobby with my mom. She told me "Have a seat." She then asked if I understood what was going on.

An older white lady walked up and said, "Hi are you, Raylene?" "Yes," I said. The older white lady had a head full of grey hair. She begins to walk to me saying she was concerned about my wellbeing. She then proceeded to tell me what was going on as far as the line of questioning she would be doing. Her biggest concerns were if I was ok and healthy. Wanted to know if I was taking care of and if I was happy. I assured her I was incredibly happy. She explained that she received a call that I was being neglected and abused.

I assured her that I was not being neglected nor abused who me? By the time she left this place she was going to be convinced I was good. She said, "I was specifically told by a staff member that I was kicked out of my home with my daughter."

Again, I lied and told her that I was never kicked out my mom would never do such a thing. I assured her I and my daughter were simply fine. She needed to know for certain if I and my daughter were together, and I say yes.

I mean it wasn't really a lie she was going to be with me after I left here so heck yea we together. She tried to get me to be honest I know she knew that I was scared. She was told by the very person I spoke to. Her facts were apparently on point. She told me ok and that I was free to go. I walked into the waiting room and told my mom we were free to go.

I remember it was raining outside and I was so excited. Could not wait to get out of that place and go see my child. I said are we going to go get T now? She was like Raylene I am sorry, but I cannot let you have her. Where are you going to stay tonight until your bus leaves in the morning, she asked? What, hold on

pump your breaks I wanted to scream. She continued, " Do you have somewhere to go. Do I have somewhere to go? I would like to go see my child. I can come to pick you up and take you back to the bus station in the morning. Wait what," I cannot even see her?" I asked. I looked at this lady and like I promise I couldn't believe this.

I was like nooooo! " I just went in there and lied to the people for you. You promised!" Tears just began to roll down my face. Why would she do this she was good at tricking me into situations that I didn't see coming. Manipulating me to do things because she knew I cared and was full of compassion. Omg! Hurt is an understatement, I was simply crushed in a million fucking pieces. She replied, "There is nothing I can do the judge gave me custody and we would have to go to court."

"It's too late to go to the courts right now," she claimed. "I would let you see the baby, but we do not want to confuse her," I said you told me and my dad that you were going to send her back. You knew before I came down here that you had custody. Was this your plan to trick me?" I asked. "You planned this all along for me to help you keep your kids while you keep my kid from me." Like I was full of rage like anger to the highest freaking level. Really this is where we are at for real? "Why are you doing this you just want everyone to think I am this fast girl out here having sex and living this horrible life."

"Why do you want my child so bad?" I asked.

As I think about this story that I write it brings so much anxiety. Pain, emotions man I felt like I had been betrayed.

Why trick and treat me like this so bad? Why have me? Look if I was going to have to treat my kid so bad and show no love, I rather not have that baby. No harm no foul, just saying. Shucks, I felt like if my mom does not like me, I must not be shit. I can't imagine ever doing anything like this to my child. It hurt so bad my mom was so overbearing, she was stricter than strict. She

controlled every facet in my life. She controlled when we talked and at what level of emotion we spoke.

I felt trapped and unloved by everyone even me. How had I just helped this lady hurt me? Trust for people period was gone at that point. I was 16 years old I didn't think nobody cared, so I stopped caring. Period! Just gave up on me. I was rejected repeatedly by my mom, peers at school, people at church. So, I learned to reject myself to eventually, I blamed myself for all these events. My mom's use of manipulation causes my self-esteem to diminish. She rejected me by not showing affection or love to me. Because of this rejection, I also dealt with chronic self-doubt. Seeing these behaviors day after day, I guess I begin to mimic them. I learned behaviors from the adults in my life.

I wondered when my mom and her friends got together why she was never approached. Maybe they were intimidated by my mom I am unsure. Not even just the previous stated behaviors, my mom also used guilt. She would use guilt trips on me a lot and make me feel like everything was my fault. Guilt is an immensely powerful weapon when used skillfully. It's like a person makes it overly clear why they are disappointed about something.

Then act like you need to find a way to fix this problem. It's not healthy communication. It is just as bad as giving someone silent treatment as a form of punishment. When a person doesn't care how their behavior affects you that is a big Red flag.

Children growing up can be very vulnerable to parents who use guilt as a form of manipulation. This can be easily done by parents, teachers anyone in a position of control. There were lots of toxic factors at play with my relationship with my mother. I hated adults because of her. I thought they were all like her I vowed when I became an adult, I would not be the reason a kid wanted to die. I cried all the way back to Delaware mentally I don't think I have ever been the same since that day.

I was all I had I must protect myself.

CITY LIFE

I had no friends, who knew me in this big ass city with all these people.

Scared but never let anyone see that. Was not from the city but learned that I had to protect myself and keep my head on a swivel. Could not be so relaxed and calm rather I had to adjust to a harsher reality altogether. My dad was genuinely mad at my mom because I was sad, and he had put steps into a plan for the care of my daughter. I believe I developed separation anxiety during this phase of my life. I didn't know how to cope I smiled beautifully on the outside. Inside I was something I cannot really explain in words.

My heart was broken what I knew as normal was gone forever never to come back. In VA. I was on a leash, couldn't even go to the gym that was right across the street from my house. In Delaware lord, I had no supervision, no rules at all. Other than not having my child this was amazing! City life was so much faster than what I had been accustomed to. The streets were narrower, and one block might have 60 homes. All lined up in rows connected. Even the stores were connected and some restaurants. The streets were all numbered and there were different sections of town that I had to learn.

I love the fast pace how everyone seemed to always be in a rush. There was always something going on the city blocks. I call it live entertainment, didn't have to wait too long for good comedy. Most of the time it was right next door. They walked, talked, and even ate fast. Whatever, I could be exaggerating a bit. It was almost as if I had been warped to the future. I was the opposite of Troy, I know yaw seen Crooklyn, right? Remember when Troy went to Va. in the movie how it went from one screen to the widescreen. She wasn't used to VA. and I wasn't used to the city. That is the best visual I can give you.

Had life always been like this for the people that lived here? I loved it; it was like a whole new world. Like so many people everywhere, so many tall buildings everything was so close. Virginia was an exceptionally clean place, but not here. Bums and drunks were everywhere. Addicts up and down the street all over, trying to sell merch. Looking horrible but I promise they did not even care. The houses were so close that they were all touching. There were stores on every corner. Liquor stores appeared to be on every other corner. Baggies covered the ground from drugs sale and the smell of weed and dirt filled the air.

No, I do not want to buy a Mr. Potato head, my kid will not play with that, I have to remind the addicts trying to sell merchandise for a hit. Loud music playing, people sitting on their porches playing cards and drinking beers. Buses trains it was almost like I was in a dream. The teens in the city seemed to have a totally different responsibility that made them more mature. Street smart with regular smart. I know I didn't have to explain that like that. They just seemed like were way more mature than me and my peers in VA. The city life was no comparison to the country's rural life in Va.

No, I wasn't raised on a farm with pigs, sheep, and goats. As they all seemed to think it was just rural family community inspired. I went from being calm to jumping into the mix of things. I had to adapt and blend in, lots of skills were learned. There was no one to show me how to adjust to living in the city but my sister definitely tried to help.

She and I were the same age, my dad swore we would be the death of him. How did he manage to have two daughters born in 75, lol? We developed a bond between me and my sister over the years. While I was in VA, we were pen pals. When we got more familiar, we would lie and tell everyone that we were a month apart. Daddy always said we were trying to make him look like a hoe. I mean in my defense he did tell me and my sister the only reason we were here is that our moms did not swallow.

Listen daddy was fun. I love my dad and miss him so much. He passed a couple of years back the most difficult pain I endured as an adult. I will talk about that later or in another book. I smile every time I think about him. He and I had way more in common than I ever realized. Love you Dad. S.I.P. Me and daddy did not always have that love relationship. Much trial and error, arguments, anger, healing, and growth. Both I and my sister were born in 75 truth is I was the oldest born in July and my sister in November. We were so excited to have each other it's like we needed each other at that time for so many reasons. She needed a sister/friend, and I needed a friend that was a sister.

We were a lot alike in some ways and even different in more. My first day in the city we turned up I never will forget. After my dad had driven all around the city introducing me to random people, he said it was time for my sister to come home. My dad surprised her didn't tell her I was there, and he said she is about to be out of school. He wanted me to walk up to her when she got off the bus to see if she would recognize me. So, we parked across the street when she got off the bus my dad said, "There she is." I got out of the car and walked upon her. She looked the same way I remember when I was 7. She was just taller, longer how every you see it plus we sent each other many pictures since we were pen pals. When I walked up to her, she was like "Raylene? What are you doing here?" Before I could respond she said. "Hold on we got to get rid of daddy it's about to be a fight."

Lol So my dad looking from the distance in the car was feeling as if she had brushed me off. He couldn't see what we were saying I guess it appeared as if she wasn't interested and my dad got out of the car. He was like, you know who that is?" "Yes," she replied, "That is my sister." She was like "Daddy me and Ray bout to go we will catch up with you later." He just looked at us and shook his head. Became one of his usual body gestures when dealing with me and her.

Daddy was like, "Excuse me."

Got back inside the car and dipped. Mane, so me and her catch up with her homegirl who is about to fight this girl by the bridge.

I will never forget the girls began to fight and I was admiring the architectural structures of the city so amazing I remember saying. The view from the bridge was genuinely nice. I thought if I were a photographer, I would capture such architectural structures of cities. Well, it appeared my sisters' friend was losing the fight.

So, I gave her the knife that I had stashed in my pant leg. I was trying to help she was getting pounded. Explain to me how she got my knife taken and got stabbed in the leg with it. Oh, my

goodness what the heck just happened. My sister grabbed her friend's left arm I grabbed the right. So much blood was coming out of her leg that we had to carry her.

The girl that stabbed her ran

off over the bridge.

I was like, "How the heck did you let her get the knife?" Dang SMH, how did we go from the fight to this. I swear I wasn't ready. This was the most action I had seen up close and personal, other than school fights happening in Va. which I was usually the entertainment. My sister was like "Man, we good as long as daddy doesn't show up. "I was like we told him we were going to chill he left".

She was like "No daddies still in the area he not going to go too far you just got here!" So, mind you, we are trying to walk up the hill carrying this young lady who is bleeding from her leg. We were having to go to 6th street which was 2 blocks up. Man, I don't know how to explain what happened next. I just know my dad pulled up my sister said, "There go daddy." We all froze I mean even the girl who got stabbed. My dad said, "What are yaw doing." My sister was like "Nothing daddy we just walking her home."

He was like, "Is that blood? Is she bleeding?" Yep, we were busted he put us in the car fussing us out as we drove to the girls' house. He wondered what made us think we could clean this up without a hospital. Either way, the girl's mom didn't have a car, so we drove them to the hospital.

The girl's mom and my dad had gone to school together, so it wasn't that bad. Well, that is until the police showed up and wanted to know where the hell the knife came from that she had been stabbed with. Our stories were totally not rehearsed lol. My dad saw right through that bs. Ha ha.... He was like "Was it your knife and why did you have a knife on you" ... lol "For protection." I told him he laughed so hard.

He was like "Why I have two 16-year old's they going to be the death of me."

That was just the first day, not even the entire 24 hours. Life daily was a whole other situation. I enjoyed it I love a great adventure, and this definitely was adventurous. Felt like a kid trapped in the house and finally allowed to go outside. Look at me, I have been set free. No more boring evenings after school reading books.

Things had just got real in my world. I was not good at faking anything for too long I could act but not that good. I stuck out like a sore thumb. The style of clothes and swag was just so different. I quickly adapted to my surroundings thanks to having a sister that was the same age as me. She also knew that I had been in VA the whole time.

The things with sisters are, I have so many I just try to be fair.

I am however super closer with others and some not so much, ever. How I figure you just love and receive love unless jealousy or envy is allowed. Other than that, I believe I am good with all my sisters now.

If we don't talk in 2020, I promise it's not my fault. I felt like an outsider so I could not have a favorite but if I could pick one it would be her. She made sure I had fun. Life for me as you read earlier was complicated as hell. The universe put her in my life to show me a great time.

You know when I lived in VA, I was the oldest the responsible one. Here I did not have to be responsible for anyone but me.

How about barely was doing a good job of that.

I thought I could handle it; I had no choice but to give it the best I absolutely could. So, I would say I became more mature. Every experience that I faced while living in Delaware matured me for what was to come in my life. Just learning how to cope was the lesson I began to learn quickly, how to make it with not one person in your corner.

Yes, my dad was there however, at 16 I had pretty much been raised. Already set in my ways not trying to budge. Seem like soon as I got with my dad it would have been love Luv. No, I had a little resentment towards my dad.

As much as I was happy to be with him, I was just as angry that he left me all those years with my mom. Had she in fact been correct? Did he not want me and if he did why not reach out? Why had he let her be the decision-maker in what happened in my life? These were not all of the role models in my life just the most influential I would say. They were mom and dad specifically; every child wants to know their parents. We watch them learn their likes and dislikes. What makes them happy and sad, how to get what you want from them, and so on. I was trying to love them, learn them, and understand the behaviors that I

saw from each of them. As I kid, I thought my parents and other adult behaviors were what I should imitate. Not needing the attention of an infant, so my dad did him. I was taking care of myself, for the most part. He let me be me he had his own life he was living before I came along. He had women and plenty of women, there was never any lack in daddy's life.

He had single women, businesswomen, women of different races. Big women, little women pretty women, and a couple of interesting choices that just make you look. I felt crazy trying to hold one dude down when my dad was juggling say, 5 women. These were grown women not little girls. I mean I won't go their daddy would get me anyway. Those were the ones I knew about anyway each woman just assumed that she was the only one.

Shucks, I was right along with them. When we would go see them, I would just assume that he was either meeting a family member or you know doing business. In Virginia I grew up in a two-parent home my dad wasn't about that life. My dad definitely was not married or was he. That was what I thought, so oh well. He was living his best life before I understood what that was. He would go to a business office and a lady would come out.

The whole time they may just be talking and then they grab a real tight hug and kiss. MMMMhhhh.... Yeah, that was my dad, and on to the next. We might go to someone's house and he lives there. Listen, I cannot make this stuff up. He might be getting fussed out for working and being gone this whole time. We chatted a lot with me and my dad like best friends. I would be like how do you not get caught? Daddy was quite the ladies' man.

They loved him, I mean who can blame them he was handsome and looked like me. Or I like him. Either way, we might go across town and see another chick. My sis and I would ask each other how we would ever be able to trust dudes. Knowing what we saw our dad do set us up to think that this was the norm for couples. My dad had all these women feeling so special that they

each learned how to cope with his schedule to be in his life. I plead the 5 on any of the stories that he ever told I was in no way....

Just a little humor. Honestly, we watched my dad live this way every day. The only problem I had was accidentally calling someone somebody else's name. Would we ever believe we were the only girl a guy was in love with? Yeah, nope I am unsure about that mostly in part to us having a firsthand look. A firsthand look to one on one male and female relations big pippin style.

However, if I could have all those different people. I would do it differently they would know about each other or we would just be open. I would not want anyone to feel that they were in for a bad surprise. I do not do well with that type ish.

Now it is just me against the world, I thought having a baby was opening my eyes.

Painfully labor did do something damaging

and absolutely amazing at the same dam time.

Moving 4 hours away to Wilmington, De changed me and well that's what opened my eyes.

LIFE WILL NEVER BE THE SAME

When my mom told stories about Delaware, they were always either bad or sad. Who would want to be someplace that a person describes as a bad scary mean place? In my mind, I was like you couldn't survive there but you want me to. That was a little weird to me beings that she was an adult who made that decision, and I was a child. Mommy was raised in Christiana, De which was a little desolate I believe?

I mean she is always talking about well water and walking miles in the snow. Yaw know them stories that our parents be telling of the old days. Christiana, Delaware which is south of Wilmington, De. was a totally different environment altogether. Because of the differences in the cities, I get why Wilmington might have been a bit much for my mom. Never did I ever understand unfortunately why I was sent to a place which she feared for her life. Those were her words though she had to go like she could not live in Delaware she had seen too much.

She said that life was not for her. There is a lot that can happen in a city, people want to relax in their adult years not have to watch your back constantly in the city.

When I bring friends up north, I will just be like stay on guard. Keep your head on a swivel you just never know. I learned that living in the city you must watch what people do, not what they say. Watch responses, body language. I could usually tell within 5 min of being in someone's presence what type of person one was. Just because I had no one teach me what to look for in people that I deal with. So, I watch everything, I probably act like I'm not paying attention or analyzing but you have been read.

Now am I to understand that my punishment was going where she felt was unsafe, dangerous, and unprotected. The good thing about me was I had a sister twin. I had a sister that was the exact age that could help me get to know the city and not stick out so bad. That was a bonus, having someone old enough to help look out for me.

She helped me fit in well except for my accent lol. Between her and her mom, I was able to find a couple of stylists to do my hair and keep me tight. It was like a community of people and they all like helping each other and functioned normally.

Just at a faster pace and more Pit bulldog fight in them. They kept you on your toes, so daddy took me shopping and fixed my wardrobe and shoe game. It really took a long time for anyone to believe I was born there. My southern accent was usually a fun topic, but everyone genuinely liked me almost as if I belonged. They loved for me to say 10, and sand and when. They would laugh

every time I opened my mouth. I was accessible to way more things than I could have ever imagined. A whole new world where things were almost opposite of the other world I lived in before.

Everything was up close and personal. Corner stores on almost every corner and where there wasn't a corner store, or a house was a liquor store. Food was even different in the city, instead of like fast-food restaurants they had more mom-and-pop shops. When it came to boys, I was fresh meat, and it was more guys than I could imagine dating. I was in teenage heaven or so it seemed.

It was almost as if I had gone thru hell but got lifted to heaven just for a minute.

I kept busy doing mischievous things along with all the other crazy kids in the city. It was more children in the city than I had ever seen in my old community. There were so many people in the city if I got tired of one, I'd just go find someone on the next block. My world would never be the same from this moment. Sometimes I was hands deep in some situations before I even knew what was going on.

I was never a shy person, so I embraced city life. When I lived back home as a child was, I had to be quiet. Children were to be seen and not heard. Those rules did not apply anymore, up here at 16 I could talk as much as everybody else. My opinion was valuable to the conversations and debates that people had.

That was the norm for most homes not all. If I could describe the difference it would be maybe basic is a word, I could use to describe it. My life in Delaware was exotic like I leveled up, I was definitely a little behind, totally comfortable in the sex department, but I was eager to learn everything we could do with our bodies. There were things teens did here that I had never heard of. So funny cause as I think back, I was the friend who had never tried a lot. They were all like you never did this ummmm.... NO, I would reply and some-things I did try others I did not.

Another thing that the city had a lot of was drugs. I was scared to do drugs because of the content commercials this is your brain on drugs with the fried egg. Baby, but Oh, there was plenty of anything and everything, every dam where. You never have to look for weed lol. Weed looks for you. Go to the corner store to get a breakfast sandwich and a bag of weed. At least that was my schedule anytime I was in the city. I spent a lot of time in Wilmington and Philadelphia or Philly as we call it. Philly was 20 min away and it was even faster than Delaware. Everything was accessible to you the cops acted as if they didn't care or it was too much to handle. Or maybe a lot

of the cops were just crooked, they never seemed to see what was apparently going on right in their face. Drought where?

Alcohol though was a whole other subject. I could not buy it but all the junkies in the city could. They could and they would for anything, even pennies lol. I could talk them into getting me a drink. Plus, it might have been wrong but the adults who I will name nameless here and deceased. S.I.P. They got me Jack Daniels wine coolers and such.

Not my dad he didn't allow this drinking. Life was real and the weather was cold and harsh in the winters. Lots of snow all over the ground. I absolutely love the snow and there is nothing you can say about it to change my mind. That is until it turns all black and the temperature drops.

Let me tell you. High School in the city was cool.

There were so many different people and different personalities you know I made friends. Do not remember too many only those that I considered my sisters. I would love to tell you guys that this story has such a happy ending at this point. However, that is not the case. My dad did not really have his own... place. He had a lady that I met that lived on the Eastside, there was another that lived on the hill and down on like 4,5 or 6th street.

There was another on Northside, I mean listen daddy had many chicks I am not exaggerating about this topic either.

All their homes were always accessible pretty much. It was just me and them getting along and the fact that I do not kiss ass well. I sort of felt like they did.

These women did not have to put up with my mess, but they did. I felt like they kissed ass because they would do anything to be with my dad. Never wanted to be like them but boy did I have a lot of things to learn.

After being in the city for a while I began to sound like them for the most part and when I spoke to my family in VA, they felt I sounded different. It is possible, I had begun to adapt, adjust to the lifestyle. I was going to school I had got signed up for school on the eastside because daddy main girl lived there. 9th and Bennett. My sister lived on the Westside and all our friends.

Daddy had another chick on that side of town which was cool and convenient. Plus, she and I got along way better than the other girlfriend.

She was a little uptight, but she was a working chick. She was

always at work or home cause the neighborhoods be kind of ruff...
rough! On the hill, it was considered bad but that was up the block
well at the end of the block so, for the most part, we were cool.

I and my sister thought it was a good idea for me to move in with
this girlfriend and just find out which bus from my school went
close. That is what I did such a breeze. My dad knew so many people I was able to get hired at McDonald's by Adams 4. The first-
ever place that hired me. I loved that job ate everything that was
on the menu that I could try. Working in the drive-thru was amazing I would always play on the speaker. I would play on the microphone and say, "Welcome to McDonald's would you like to try our
new Turkey legs?

We would clown get the people to agree, wait till they get to the
window act like management, and say we were sold out. Money was
good beings though I was supporting myself. Daddy would get ghost
and then come back randomly. For the most part, he knew I was in
one place or another. Yeah, I would say shelter, on the other hand,
was a big issue.

If daddy and this chick get to arguing about another chick, she
does not want us around. Neither did he want to be around someone he was constantly arguing with, so you know he just goes to the
next chick's house.

Sometimes I may not be around in a heated argument and get off
and cannot get in the house and must walk around.

Was not such a big deal as there were usually people outside all
night. I got kicked out of school in the 11th grade because of my address. Not only would daddy and his girlfriend get in arguments, so
would we. I remember one day at one of his girlfriend's house she
told me he walked out the door and went one way and I went the
other. The address situation was nothing to play with, within the
Delaware school system. I got kicked out of school until I could pro-

vide proof of address. Daddy didn't have proof of address that was his own.

Sometimes I think like because I was getting kicked out, he might have made peace with a chick for a place. Then it was trial and error. My dad was a good man and like my mom, I loved him to pieces, but he was neglecting me. Regardless of how I dress it up, he was uninvolved clearly in my life. My dad had custody of me according to the courts. It's kind of funny I feel like I really had custody of myself.

It was me who made sure I had food, clothing, and shelter. When a parent focuses more on their own problems and desires. They tend to focus little time on their child, and everything comes before that kid. My dad wasn't really emotionally attached to me either. Out of this, I ended up being an emotionally needy person. I never knew that I was being neglected by my dad until years later. I thought I was selfish because I wanted more of my dad's time than I was being given.

When children deal with neglect during childhood it disrupts how their brain develops. The way they process information gets kind of fuzzy. I suffer from isolation, fear, and an inability to trust anyone. These are all effects of being neglected. Abuse is the intentional infliction of harm on someone, whether it is physical, emotional, or sexual. And neglect is the failure to provide the necessary care for an individual.

It can also be a failure to act or notice a Childs emotional needs. I have all the symptoms of a child that had abusive emotionally unattached parents. Failure to thrive, aggressiveness, and shunning emotional intimacy. I always wondered why my dad never came to Virginia to rescue me. Even if he did have a life that was busy why reject me?

When I needed my dad the most, he was absent, nowhere to be found. His love I wondered about too; not sure he cares for me either. Seemed like my mom was doing all the damage but they both played a part. They were the parents, and their child was suffering.

It's ok I learned to rely on myself for everything. I do blame my dad for his share of parenting. What was in his control that he didn't do?

Cause as a teenager both of my parents caused some form of pain, nobody loved me nobody cared. I should have been able to rely on both of my parents for emotional stability and all my other needs. Where one lacked the other should have been there to make sure I was ok. Truth be told I think both my parents were broken. If you draw a box and then scribble inside that's what I felt like on the inside.

CHOICES AND DECISIONS

End of the school year the truancy officers had finally caught up with me. I knew they were looking for me I was ducking them. Another student told me that if that particular guy was looking for me, he was a truancy officer. Could not imagine why a truancy officer was looking for me, I was in school every day. The last week of school on a Thursday my running was about to come to an end. Me and a friend were skipping class in the cafeteria. One of my homies had called my name in the hall.

When I turned around, he was like there she goes, and the truancy officer walked up to me. He said, "You are a mighty hard person to catch up with, I been looking for you." Couldn't run anymore, I was caught so I had to chill and cooperate with the man. He wanted me to come to his office so we could talk privately since I was with friends. He explained he had been looking for me since I changed bus stops from the east side to the west. They said the address that I lived at on the east side had sent mail back.

So, the school must have sent some mail to my dad's girlfriend's house and she must have sent it back. The school pays attention to all mail returned because usually, this is the way the school communicates with your family. Anytime mail is sent back with a return to sender truancy takes over to get answers needed. In a nutshell that is why they had been looking for me. They could not reach my parents. He needed my dad to show proof that I lived on the west side to continue going to school and riding that bus.

the other option was, I had to have proof that I lived on the east-side. Then I would have to go back on the east side and ride my correct bus. The east side was its own little world. I rode the bus over there maybe two weeks, possibly a month. All the other days I rode the bus from the west side. I liked my dad's girlfriend on that side of town plus she was just a couple of years older than me so I could relate to her.

It was the end of the school year, the only problem I faced was finding my dad before the new school year started or I would be kicked out for no address.

I felt we would figure something out by the time Sept rolled around. We had the whole summer to figure out if he wanted to keep me in this school or move me to another school. He and the east side chick were on bad terms. I'm not sure what had caused the breakup. However, because their relationship ended, she sent all our mail away. Good thing for me I still had my job at McDonald's thru all of this. during the summer I worked as many hours as could get.

I was a good employee at McDonald's, so I got lots of hours. When we closed the store, we would

play too much and get on the manager's nerves. "Clock out get off my clock" the manager would yell. Fun stuff, I tried to get us to stay for as long as I could, the reason is when I got off, I did not have anywhere to lay my head.

So, I would walk some nights from 2 am until at least 7 when it seemed ok to knock on someone's door. I would see who was outside I knew if people were out it was cool if not it was lonely, to say the least. Early at 7 am I knew my sister's grandmother would be up so I would go over there. I'd knock on the door and she would want to know why I was up so early. I would make up something say my sister was expecting me and she would let me in. I would go upstairs to the second floor and climb into the bed with my sister. I was safe I made it another night alive, yeah me.

For the most part, I was ok and comfortable, so my dad was doing his usual self. The summer was so fun every kid around seemed to be daredevils. Everything we did we probably should not have been doing. During the summer school was out we were on summer break I spent a lot of time with my sister, so my dad wasn't worried.

There was so much to get into in the city, house parties which I loved. Clubs, block parties the vibe of the environment was enjoyable.

There were times when my sister would bump heads with her mom. She might not be allowed to hang out, they would fight, and I would have to rescue her. I would call one of my other aunts to come help and when all else failed. Just call daddy, tell him to meet me at the corner by my sisters' house. He did and he would go to her mom's house and tell her we had some family stuff going on and he needed her. Her mom would say ok maybe not so easy as it sounds. She did allow her to be with daddy because he came over. Daddy would let my sister gather her things then walk her to the corner where I was. We would go one direction and he would go the other. Mission accomplished!

That summer while at work I had met a guy. He lived with his mom and he would sneak me in, she did not want me there. I ended up getting pregnant that summer after moving in with my boyfriend. Once his mom found out I was pregnant she allowed me to stay. She had gone to school with my dad as well and liked him. So, she requested to meet him to allow me to continue to stay at her house. I felt that was fair enough.

I mean I was turning 17 soon when I tested positive on my pregnancy test. I and my baby father were no good in a relationship, so we cut our losses and went our separate ways. Honestly, then I went from pillar to post as they call it. I had to make some decisions on what I was going to do with my life and now about to be a mom again. I do not know if I was ready, but I was definitely having mixed feelings about being pregnant.

I wanted a baby, missed my own baby, on top of those crazy emotions I was homeless. Real shit, I did not even know where I was going to lay my head most nights. I remember hanging out with friends and they use to sneak me in their bedroom windows so they wouldn't get caught because they didn't want me walking the streets all night.

Kids trying to be simply great humans in our own little world. Waking up early in the morning before their

parents had to go to work somedays. I was so thankful for my girlfriends. I'm not really sure what was more embarrassing not having a place to stay or sleep on my friend's shoes in their closet.

I remember one night I wanted to go out on a date, me and my sister would double date. I had two guys from the hood that wanted to take us out and I couldn't find her.

I waited all night called her mom and everyone in our little click like let her know I am looking for her. I never found her that night, but I thought I would, so I decided to go ahead and tell the guys to come on over. So, they came over and took me for a ride with them, we drove around to the spots I thought my sister might be. We never found her, so they decided to make a stop at someone's sister's house. I told them I would stay in the car until they came out, but they insisted that I come inside.

For whatever reason, I felt a little scared to go into the house but I thought there is a lady there so I should be ok. The lady was upstairs she never even came downstairs, but I did hear her. A few minutes later things took a turn for the worse. I was raped that night by those 2 dudes. I cannot lie it was a bad situation, but I caused it. Everything in me knew that getting in that car without my sister was wrong and I still did it. Some things you begin to realize when healing. You look at your life to gain understanding.

You are in control of your life unexpected things are different some things you have more control over than you give yourself credit for, I do not look to blame people I just look to get understanding. To heal I know I must be honest with myself first, no one can heal until they learn to be honest with themselves.

No, I did not ask to be raped and yes rape is wrong. However, if

I am, to be honest, Raylene, put herself in a situation that was not good.

Again, every cause affects.

The situation would have never happened if I had waited for my sister or just not chose to go. Things would have gone completely different. The choice I made put me in a situation that hurt me and could have hurt me way worse. In all actuality, I am blessed to come out alive and with my right mind. I do not think when women are raped it's always something they did. I just know what happened to me and I put myself in that situation. Yes, I am a survivor of rape, not a victim, there is a difference.

I felt uncomfortable as hell there I did not want to be there. Dang, I should have just stayed at home I told myself. Maybe that was a sign that I should not go out with these knuckleheads. The atmosphere in the house just changed that's all I know. Some things went down maybe I will write about that next, but I am not about to get all into that.

One then another over and over again until I was raped repeatedly. I was threatened with a gun, so I did not argue too much. I might not try to open my mouth when they want me to perform oral sex on them. That was the best resistance that I had at that specific time. In the end, they won they had the weapon to make me stay in line and I did. That was probably physically the worst thing that

had happened to my body. I felt like they took my body away from me in a way that I may not be able to get back. I always wondered what I did to make them feel this was ok. Probably nothing at all I just should not have been there. I never said I wanted sex, we never discussed it. We did not really talk about much come to think of it.

They just did things to my body that I didn't ask for. but I knew it wasn't right. Hard to explain how my little mind took that all in. I just knew that I should be able to say who could and couldn't enter my body. My self-esteem took another hit, I blamed myself for not being able to control the situation. Like I had to be my own mom, sounds nuts but true. I had boundaries growing up I could have got raped if I were in VA, and I had made the same crazy choices. All men are not bad I don't feel that way. Not sure how I feel about those guys who had raped me.

Just wondered how they would feel if someone did what they did to me to their daughter, mom, or sister. I eventually told my dad he was sad, and he wanted to prosecute them, but I told him I'd never testified. Could not deal with an attorney questioning and making me look like a fool for my bad decisions. Some of the adult women in my life for the most part fussed me out for being there and hugged me tight cause they wanted me to be ok. One day I and one of my homegirls were on the west side and I thought I saw the guys ride past. We were talking and I just froze when I saw them, I did not want to make eye contact. They saw me anyway, my home-girl noticed my body language and was like who are they in that car. I told her those are the guys that raped me.

They pulled up by the steps, "Hey what you are doing tonight is this your sister" they asked. I never replied my friend was like "Get away from her she does not want to be bothered and she is not going anywhere with yaw perverts." My friend said, "Matter of fact I think yaw need to leave before I call the police for rape." The guys looked at her and walked away got back in their car and left. Over the year's life took a toll and me and my homegirl went different paths. I was never able to let her know that I needed her that night, and she came thru for me. Didn't know she was going to stand up for me like that, but I needed her, and she came thru for me.

SUPPRESSING FEELINGS

God,

> *grant me the Serenity,*

>> *to accept the things,*

I cannot change,

> *the Courage to*

>> *change the things*

I can and

> *the Wisdom*

>> *to know*

the difference

AMEN!

When my sister found out what occurred with me that night, she was hurt. We had been doing a great job so far of taking care of each other. She kept me out of trouble, I kept her out of trouble. If she was doing the most or drunk, I had her. If I was drunk and out of it, she had my back. We would be in situations where guys would be ready to have sex with one of us, the other would have to be the cock blocker.

Codes and signals to let each other know what we needed to happen. If we didn't want to have sex, we were on our periods. This one dude said, "You been on your period longer than any girl I know." We would laugh so hard out of what we felt were desperate situations.

If nobody cared that we were alive, we cared for each other, nothing else came first when we were on some sister ish.

From the time I got to Delaware until the day I left, she was consistent in my life. We were more than just sisters we were friends. Most days we were all we had; she was devastated when she found out. "Why didn't you just wait for me?" She asked.

However, I couldn't answer that question because I really didn't have an answer. She knew if we were together that would never happen. I am my sister's keeper; this was indeed how my dad had us behave. He really didn't care what the facts were that lead up to the event, he just needed to know, we had each other's back.

We were always together like shadows, sometimes I thought she got tired of me because I had to follow her around like a baby. Only because I was still learning the city, she never made me feel like a burden, trust she had her own drama going on. She was like my guardian angel and I was hers. We both suppressed our feelings, not the best behavior to handle anything. We were similar when it came to a lot of our behaviors. Both our parents were a lot alike to a certain degree I bet if they tested us, we might have some of the same childhood issues. Like I said we were both suppressing our feelings about how we felt. When it came to this situation, I totally put a lid on it.

Rape, how do I just talk about that, it was ok with me if it was never brought up again. However, for me to grow, I had to learn to deal with how I felt about being raped. I don't think suppression was the right way to handle all situations. For some reason, I felt it was appropriate for this story. Once I can talk about it without force, I can heal. There were better ways to deal with this situation like express my emotions.

That was something altogether, that I was not about to let happen.

However, over the years I had become incredibly good at suppressing my feelings. This was a learned behavior and my go-to for most situations that I faced. Nobody was paying attention anyway to my feelings, not even me. I did not have time to deal with the effects of the rape.

There was nothing I was doing in my life that could fix this. What is done is done, there were more important things to maybe figure out. Like where I might be staying tonight. Or if I could hustle up enough money to feed myself if nobody had food for me.

Such as most events in my life there was no time to focus on the problems that came. The best solution for me was to delay dealing with the matter, until further notice.

The way I figured I didn't have time to deal with this particular emotion right now. So, I'll just ignore it altogether since I don't have the power to fix it. Rejecting my own beautiful self. This behavior taught me to become an introvert.

For the most part, my personality was that of an extrovert. Holding in my emotions which is known as suppressing emotions caused a physical strain on my body. I did not know this though; didn't have a clue I was hurting me like everyone else. Any emotion, be it grief, sadness, depression they all lead to physical stress, especially when you let it sit and just grow.

People always say look on the bright side.

Bet you never know that in difficult times that's very unhealthy behavior. My favorite line to everyone is no worries, part of my daily vocabulary. When you suppress your feelings and keep them bottled up it does not stop you from feeling them. You just choose to ignore them but why?

Wouldn't it be better to talk about the problem regardless of the outcome? I can agree that sometimes talking during difficult issues is not easy. You must allow the emotion to happen which can be a very painful process, cry about it, learn from it whatever effect it brings. Studies also show that avoiding emotions can lead to problems with depression, anxiety, and aggression.

I was so explosive, not sure how to give you an example!

It was horrible, I overreacted to situations that I probably should not have been so hurt or angered over. Snapping out was normally part of my personality because emotions were particularly important, and I wasn't actually using them. When you don't use your emotions, you are then handicapping them or maybe even holding them hostage. Our emotions help us act, strike and avoid danger, survive, make decisions and understand things around us. When we suppress the emotion, we are not allowing them to show us how to act. Emotions allow us to respond appropriately and build deeper relationships.

They allow us to communicate effectively. So of course, if I was suppressing my emotions, I was not expressing them correctly.

The only way that I could have expressed my emotions correctly would have been to accept them and deal with the situation so I could move on. Not me, I was indeed a firecracker, always ready to blow. I never took the time to understand the emotions behind how I was feeling. Why was I really acting this way? Other people's perspectives didn't matter because I felt they didn't care about mine; I took a lot of stuff personally.

Truth be told I am not totally healed to this day from some of these things.

Now that I am older, I simply better know how to handle myself in certain situations. What I learned in my journey is if you ever tried to push away a feeling or thought, then you were suppressing it. We all do things to get rid of these feelings, some turn to alcohol and drink or do drugs, while others do mediation techniques to help make them relax. We all choose a coping mechanism whether good or bad, suppressing emotions is just the one I chose.

I was scared to do drugs; I have never done any drugs in my life. I do smoke weed, an herb and yeah, I know smoking is bad for my health as well. I am healing, and hopefully so are you so let's do this together and grow.

I was such a moody person and had all types of anxiety.

This cycle that I was creating was me trying to push something away that seemed to keep coming back and never go away. It's like the more I push sad thoughts away the sadder thoughts came. People would ask if I was ok. I didn't know when I replied, "No!" That at that very moment I was suppressing my emotions. I am unsure how I began to use this as a coping mechanism I just know I did always act this way.

Can't remember exactly where I learned about the face and milliseconds. But I had learned something about the fact

that it takes 100 milliseconds for a person's brain to react emotionally. Listen I don't know by heart about this milliseconds stuff. Just know I have read it several times. Stating it takes

600 milliseconds for our brain to register this reaction. By the time you decide that you don't need to be mad, you have already shown it for some milliseconds. Research it for yourself, remarkably interesting finds. Since technology has changed so much think about a text you send out of anger.

Once you hit send you can't take it back.

Yeah, deep but true. So, I learned a valuable lesson about my emotions. That they are normal, and I need to deal with them accordingly. My emotions are important if not I wouldn't have them, none of us would. Therefore, they are important cause they have a purpose.

Everything about me is important, a valuable lesson I will never forget.

The primary reason I feel I suppressed my emotions was out of fear of being disciplined or further being rejected. I displaced a lot of anger, as a child I didn't know this was what I was doing. Ignorant to the fact that I was even suppressing my feelings until late in my 20's.

To me it was normal, the whole time I was displacing anger because I couldn't direct it where it needed to go. Man, oh, man. I did not want to come across as unlikeable or negative. In such a world where people are so judgmental, I dare not look as if I was weak either.

In return, I dumped my suppressed emotions everywhere but in the correct place. Seem like I was causing more problems than I was fixing but I was a teenager. We didn't make it this far in health class ever, but we should always deal with our emotions, if you don't fix what's wrong the problem will continue to exist.

All I had to do was talk to that lady in middle school. I always felt that talking to her might have changed my life. However, now that my life has happened the way it did, I am grateful because my story can help another family or person. When I write I express my emotions?

Two of my favorite past times writing my thoughts and playing my violin.

I put this chapter in this book only to touch on the causes and effects of suppressing emotions. I am a prime example of suppressed emotions.

A very Toxic situation because when anger is not expressed appropriately it can disrupt relationships, affect thinking and behavior patterns. I was hurting myself more than I was helping myself. All my coping mechanisms were horrible for me. They weren't allowing me to grow they were holding me back from my purpose.

The coping mechanisms that I was using were extremely unhealthy. Coping means invest one's conscious effort, solving personal and interpersonal problems, to try to master stress and conflict in your life. A coping mechanism is a behavior that someone engages in to try and protect themselves from psychological damage, these mechanisms can be good or bad, healthy or unhealthy.

We all must find effective ways to deal with stressful situations. There are many ways to cope, suppressing emotions being one and a negative way to deal with stress if I may say so myself. A More positive way would be Humor. Laughing is fun and is happy and it shows all forms of positive-ness. Problem-solving is learning to locate the reason for the problem and determine a solution.

Relaxation and sports are both positive ways to deal with stress. You, me we all must figure out what works for us and do that because what works for another person may not work for you. The key to understanding yourself is figuring out what works for you, then apply it and make it work for you.

When you use positive coping mechanisms you increase resilience.

You learn how to handle negative emotions and difficult situations better.

You learn how to minimize a stressful situation.

What I needed to learn was to regulate my emotions and not suppress them. This would help my intimate relationships and lead to better health overall. I needed to look at the impact of the emotions I was having, identify what I was feeling, and embrace it.

Why not just take the time and teach me?

I had so much to learn on this road to adulthood, women-hood. Harboring negative hurtful emotions was not helping me.

If you want to live a more positive productive life you must learn to let it Go! Release your emotions. This was a big lesson for me, and one well needed.

Emotions need to be released not held in.

As always.... Each one teach one.

WANDERING SOUL

When I finally caught up with my dad, I told him I wanted to go to Job Corps. He asked if I was sure." Yes, I said because if we don't have a consistent address to use, this will be a problem again". He understood my point and agreed if this is what I really wanted. It was almost the last day I could get him in the office of the recruiter. She kept telling me the date was approaching. I needed to bring my dad to sign the paperwork. We called every number we could until we found daddy. We had almost missed it by the skin of our teeth. I needed someplace to get my education.

Contrary to what people might have believed, I loved school. Well, that there may be a bit untrue. Well, it was not really school that I liked it was learning. I am a Philomath, a lover of learning. Learning new facts and knowledge is intriguing to me. So, the thought of not being able to go to school brought anxiety also. Trying to find my dad was like trying to find a needle in the haystack. He blends in well with his surroundings.

Hence where me and my sister get that characteristic from.

My sister was going, and I found out my best friend was going so I wanted to go be with them. Plus, Job Corps had food, clothing, and shelter. This had to be the best idea I had come up with that summer. The best part was it was me and my friends I mean I had to do something I could never be a drop-out I had to push until I won.

I was not an emancipated teen by the court, so I needed my dad to sign for me to be able to get in. I got accepted to go to Job Corps in Allentown Pa. with my friends. It was so hard to find my dad to get him to get my school information. Certain things I think children should never have to worry about! Mostly where they are going to lay down their head at night.

Before we left to go to the school that summer, they had the Italian Festival. The festival was held on the West side of town.

While standing in line to get funnel cakes, I met another sister. She was my dad's wife's daughter, and I didn't know too much about her just that she was another sister. Which didn't matter either way sisters were everywhere I should never have to be lonely again. What was one more? My dad had about 6 children that we knew of and one on the way.

While we were hanging out and meeting up with friends we bumped into my brother as well. That was my first time meeting him also I was so eager to meet my brother, for years I had heard about him even from my mom. Now I was finally able to put a face to my big brother. Siblings are amazing you can never have enough siblings. I enjoyed every sibling I was ever blessed with!

We all have experienced good and bad times. I am thankful for all time spent with them. That was probably the highlight of the summer. Well not really just some memorable moments. I can't tell you what exactly the highlights of the moment were. We had way too much to get into on a warm summer night. Always doing something mischievous, like dumping trash cans on people's cars and getting chased all over town by them. letting air out of all the car tires that looked like the owners loved them. Taking the Mercedes signs off cars wearing them on our necks. Block parties, House parties, water ice stands, pool parties, Summers in the city are the best for sure hands down.

Getting ready to go to Job Corps was like being in college. We had to prepare by getting personals and packing clothing. Going to school would be far and we were expected to begone for a while. I never cared It was what I needed all in one, school and home. Keystone was the center that we were assigned to their campus was a huge job corps center.

I had so much fun over the summer, we had an adventurous time too say the least.

Job Corps was everything I expected such a cool place, there were so many kids from all over there were at least 500 kids or more there. The dorm I was in was on the corner of the street my sister and best friend were lucky enough to get picked in the same dorm.

When you are new to job corps it's like a whole new world everyone wants to know who you are and where you are from.

It was a highly creative place to be especially for someone like me with no place to call home. When we first got there, we had orientation. That is how they knew you were a recruit we had to get assigned dorm and dorm duties. We were given lockers to house our belongings as well. They gave us a tour of the center which took all day. There were lots of papers to fill out, tests and procedures for evaluations. Job Corps was a trade school with an amazing hands-on learning opportunity for kids. Took us at least a week or two to finally get settled in, it was so fun, there were kids from all over the northeast attending.

Once being there for about a month, we had to get a physical. This was the part I was worried about. Some of the other students knew that I was pregnant we begin to make friends and tell each other our life stories. My friends were saying that I needed to use someone else's urine, when getting the physical all girls were tested for pregnancy.

Job Corps like any other place had to maintain safety for all students.

Pregnant girls were considered high risk at work and school and the idea of messing with people's bodily fluids was not sanitary to me.

What was the worst that could happen? Being kicked out, I guess.

I ended up having to leave the Job Corps because I failed the pregnancy test, I knew I was pregnant before I went there. Me my sister my girlfriend had talked about it, but it was worth a try, we thought just maybe I could at least get in and get started before they found out.

I ended up getting sent back to Delaware, back at square one.

This time I decided to see if I could find my mom's people her sister did want me to come so maybe I could stay there for a while. Plus, it wasn't like I didn't want to know my mom's family. I just was not allowed to communicate with them as a youth unless my mom was around. I knew she was traumatized but they were funny to me.

I just wanted to be able to get to know them for myself and not through my mother's eyes. Figured I could pass my own judgment on whether they were good or bad for me. Don't know what would make me think that would work, my mom's family was a bit different and there were a lot of underlying issues going on that I never got to the bottom of.

My aging grandmother, I was told grandmother was now old and had extreme kidney problems, she had to take dialysis. I wasn't quite sure what it was I just knew it was a serious condition and she was dying because her kidneys were shutting down. My aunt had her own daycare business and my grandma and godmom were always over there playing spades. They didn't know I didn't have anywhere to go I would just go over there and stay as long as I could. By now I was showing, and everyone knew that I was pregnant and about to have a baby soon. I swear I felt like a big burden a life with no purpose at all is how I felt just wandering the world with no one to care and no place to call home. I just wanted to be good at something and do something worth being recognized.

When my aunt got nosey and wanted to know where I was staying, I would just make up something. I had nowhere to stay, and it was dead winter, brutally cold and harsh. Being around my grandmother and god mom I learned how to be a magnificent spades player. My grandma could read a hand of cards and tell you exactly what card you had in your hand.

Those were during fun moments that happened not too often, but I sure embraced it like I had been living this way all my life. My grandma was older, and I just felt it was a pleasure to be in her sight and suck up all her wisdom before it was too late.

However, we really didn't have a relationship and so it was hard to fake closeness, so I dare not try. I was over at one of my aunt's house a lot she would say that I could stay but to me, she was so messy. She was a little lady with a big mouth, and she talked about everyone as if she did no wrong. She talked about everyone, so I knew she was talking about me and everything I had going on. Me and my cousin were close as far as we could during that time had a lot of incest issues. One night I stayed over me, and my cousin had been up all night because I wanted to learn how to shuffle cards. It took me a whole 24 hours to learn how to shuffle cards. Enough 42 cards pick up and you learn really fast.

Either way, we didn't go to bed until like 3 am. We crashed I can't remember exactly how his room looked but I think we fell asleep with him at one end and me at another. My aunt woke us up at 5 am. She immediately began screaming at us! "I don't know what yaw think this is." She stated. "You won't use my house to do your dirty work. I don't allow incest in my home."

Incest? Wait just a freaking moment, really? Wasn't that what happened when families had sex with each other. She has got to be crazy this can't be real. Felt like I had to be dreaming because this conversation was in the way.

Strange was all I could think. Like I said my mom's side of the family had some traumatic experiences going on. I don't know or want to know all that was endured to these women as young girls. However, I wasn't sleeping with any men that I called family. Period, not now or ever! I don't even like sleeping with my cousin's friends.

They would always get mad, but I felt like they were just too close to family. My thoughts were she had to be traumatized to think we were doing this type of behavior.

Or this crazy lady was delusional. Did she really think this bad of us? I had managed to avoid these people my whole time in Delaware and when I decide to come around this was all she could think of? We were family but we were distant. My mom would not talk about it much, but I believed she hated her family.

Then we lived far so I just felt moving was my mom's way of escaping her family trauma. She didn't want to deal with her family because it was painful. So, because of this, we were distant from my mother's family members. The only reason I was even dealing with them was that I had got kicked out of my mom's house. This experience was one that I will never forget. Who just assumes incest out of all things in America?

First off, I do not fuck my family, I was raised to believe that behavior was savage. Makes you wonder what she went through, that was random as hell. People are nuts I thought. Did she really just wake us up and say this, I had heard ridiculous stories of abuse. I did not care to know the vulgar details of what happened. Since I am not a counselor, it was not mandatory, and I was fine with that. What in her mind made her think just because we fell asleep in the bed that we were fucking? She pissed me off then the next thing I know she and my cousin

had words but he was respectable.

He could not tell his mom she was being ridiculous, but I could, and I did. She and I argued and she told me to get out. Big deal my mom's family is really a whole other topic seriously for another day. I was not comfortable being there also because my aunt was always talking about her son's penis. She was obsessed if you ask me. She was always comparing his penis to all the rest of the penises in the world. "My son has a huge dick she would say."

Always talking about how big it was, what mom does that shit! There are a lot of topics when it comes to my mom's family that definitely need to be addressed. They helped me understand abuse. That abuse is real and so are the effects of abuse!

Just because you don't talk about issues doesn't mean they are not present. Things will come out one way or another if it is inside.

I left that night thankfully my sister had also come home from job corps for health issues. So, I just went to her house and crashed. I ended up cursing my aunt out again about a week later. I had forgotten my deck of cards some clothes and some of my cassette tapes, my cousin told me he had bagged up my items come get my things when I got a chance. Well because I didn't have a way to get there, I had to walk from

the west side to the north side to get my things from her home. When I got there, I knocked on the door and my grandmother and god mom were already there when I arrived. Great I thought now my aunt is going to put on a show for them and act all extra. She was very sarcastic, "And how can I help you?" I just looked at her, I said. "Your son said he left a bag for me." She claimed she didn't know what I was talking about. She was being messy as hell.

I was like listen "I walked all the way over here; big and pregnant I'm not leaving without my things." She then told me she didn't have anything of mine and if I left it there now it belonged to her. My cousin was not at the house. He had probably told me to come over and collect my things 2 weeks ago. I just didn't have a way to get it, so I went when I was able.

I said you knew I was coming all the way over here to get my things.

Before I walked all the way over there I called. The problem was my cousin was not there and she had an audience. Man, I cussed her smooth out in front of my god mom and grandmother. Yes, it was disrespectful as hell, but she deserved every bit of every word I said.

Fuck being nice I was tired of being nice to people just so I had somewhere to lay my head. She didn't want me around and I didn't want to be around her. Felt like they were all some pedophiles still to this day.

Sometimes I feel like she talked about everyone else so much as to keep the negative focus off her. I'm just a kid though what do I even know. I was not going to take my big pregnant butt to her house anymore. Not allowing her to use my situation to play the victim and run my name in the ground.

At this point in life, I was sick and tired of being homeless not having a place to call home. So, I then decided to go to Juvenile court downtown. I figured if I went in this building and told these people that I was homeless they had to help. Did not want my parents to get in any trouble. It was just too much to make sure I had a place to sleep at night. My anxiety level was exceedingly high, being an adult was hard.

Of course, I could crash at my sisters. I just hated being questioned about why I was there. It was bothersome having to always explain why I did not have anywhere to stay. My dad was no were to be found and my mom was 4 hours away. If they were parenting me, I might have a place to lay my head.

My dad didn't know I didn't have anywhere to sleep. It was not a priority of his to make sure I did either. Yes, he had many girlfriends that I could stay with. It wasn't their responsibility to take care of me, nor did I have to deal with them. Their house was not home, and it was uncomfortable cause these people were strangers.

At the end of the day if my parents couldn't do what was needed to make sure I was ok. It was my responsibility.

I was a streetwalker, and this is just not how I wanted to end my story. So, I had to figure out something and I was trying the best I knew how. Couldn't express to anyone how incredibly lonely I felt. There was no place that I felt comfortable to be I began to get accustomed to sleeping anywhere. Some nights I did not have any place to go.

I would just walk all night long around the city. When morning came, I would go to one of the locations where I had close and groom myself. If the house and occupants were relaxed and laid back.

I would take a nap maybe in another home because I wasn't allowed. If one of my friends called or came over, I would go hang out, this was my normal routine. Some homes I could go to any time of the night, but the door might be locked by the time I get off work.

Truthfully, I probably should have confided in my dad more. Our relationship was kind of set up to fail. My mom told me no good things about my dad and his family and truth be told she really didn't know his family. Everything that was directed towards them was always negative.

I still was intrigued; my personality was more than similar to my dad's.

We had like ways like there was a divine connection. We had many hearts to hearts. I never told him all of the things I endured with my mom. Whenever I would bring up situations that I experience, my dad would get upset. He apologized to me for not being there and told me he was wrong. He told me he was not stable, and he couldn't remove me from a stable home. This is where I was, then my stepdad had adopted me, once this happened my dad's rights were taken away. When I was12 my stepdad adopted me and had my last name changed to his.

He did not want me to feel different from my siblings. If anything happened to him, he wanted the world to know that I was his child too.

My mom did not contact my dad she had the ad run in a paper outside of the county. I can in no way state these as facts as I was told this story by numerous people on both sides of the family. What the motives were behind these actions, I cannot say, nor do I pretend to no. Not pointing the finger just telling my story. My aunt told me by the time she found my dad to tell him.

The adoption process had already gone through and my dad did not have any rights over me.

My dad was not even notified that I was being adopted. Truth be told I did not want to be adopted, for what it is worth, I liked my name and who I was. My name change could not even help me in any way. I tried to reach my dad myself during this adoption process I was just unsuccessful.

I didn't care what anybody in America felt my stepdad loved me, and I was his kid also. I felt special because I had two dads, I thought it was better than having one. Plus, I prayed to God that, my dad saw the ad, this must be some type of injustice. Nevertheless, I understood my stepdad's views, just felt like my dad had a voice and if he used his voice what would he say to change my situation. To me it wasn't fair however, it happened I was so sad felt like my dad and I would never have the chance to get to know each other.

From the age of 7 to 16 I only spoke to my dad twice ever. I was very eager to know him, from the moment I met him I was in love.

Once I got to Delaware, we talked a lot about a lot of things me and daddy. He was one of the few people with who I could be myself around. Like he told me he wasn't perfect, and he had issues he was an open book with me, so I was an open book with him. We talk straight up and down, no chaser, I believed him being so open was something I needed during this phase of my life. My parents were total opposites, mommy was married, a Christian missionary she didn't drink or smoke attend clubs or parties. My dad was all over the place he partied.

His life was truly being enjoyed the streets had taught him a lot more than he could ever get credit for.

My dad was an incredibly wise man and he made me think about my actions from a different place. He just didn't have his own place and before I moved there, he was everywhere.

He was living his life his way and it was working for him. In his defense he did not have to have his own place, he had a couple of different children and baby moms. This was the life he chose for himself. Really, he only had to be responsible for himself.

So, then off guard, this child whom he has no rights to is now his responsibility. No warnings at all I felt my mom used her power incorrectly. She had the power to keep me in my dad's life and to keep me away I had been adopted by another man, I know my dad was hurt by this and I think he himself gave up hope. I was snatched away for at least a decade, he probably thought I did not want to be bothered. Amongst other things, this was very much a hopeless situation, so it seemed.

To a certain degree, he was happy to have me there.

Why would he feel any other way? It all just happened before he could even begin to prepare for it. I was there in the flesh. You know the song Papa was a rolling stone Wherever he lay his hat was his home. He did not have to be solely responsible for another sole and then boom a 16-year-old with hell a lot of baggage comes into your life and you must be a daddy to a child that was taken away without your permission. These are actual events that happened.

My dad was a very laid-back dude he kept it as real with me as he could. Bluntly honest about the issues of life he could make you feel like an idiot and loved at the same dam time. Like yeah, you messed up, but did you learn anything?

He was so remarkably interesting to me.

If not, nothing's changed he would say. You're still the same and I love you just messed up, but it's not the end of the world. His sense of humor always made conversations easy to have. He was probably the only man I ever let get that close to my heart. I promise I didn't know whether I was smart or stupid by the time I finish talking to my dad. He had a way with words he never lied to me about anything I asked him. Just because I was his daughter, he didn't give me any breaks

I admired him for the way he talked to me, he was easy like Sunday morning. When I was wrong, he told me I was wrong, if I did something stupid, he told me it was stupid, but he showed love even in correction.

I was never physically disciplined by my dad. His tongue was sharp, and his words cut deep. He had the ability to give you great insight on a subject without making you defensive. Whether it was his tone of voice or just adult wisdom he could get to me. Have me feeling like an idiot then tell me there's no reason to be all sad, what is done is done. Any question in the world I wanted to know the answers to, he'd answer, my dad's life was just as easy as him.

He was in a relationship with most of his children's moms. So, he never needed his own place until I came along. Then things got real plus he was fighting his own demons.

Regardless of the facts, this was no way for me to be living and I deserved better.

NO PLACE TO CALL HOME

When I went to Juvenile court I asked to speak to a worker. The lady asked me what I needed, and I told her a place to sleep. She asked how old I was, and I replied 17 she asked where my parents were. I told her my mom had kicked me out and my dad was hard to reach at times. She proceeded to call my dad who did not answer the phone just like I had stated. She then told me she wanted to call my mom. Basically, she felt that if my mom knew I was homeless she might let me come back.

I told her I doubted it because my mom was adamant that she didn't want me there. As I explained my story, I expressed I had no desire to be with her. She called my mom and told her what was going on with me in Delaware and that she worked at juvenile court. My mom told that lady that I was not her responsibility anymore, she explained that she kicked me out and that I was not allowed to be within 100 yards of her at any time.

The lady asked my mom what I do so bad that would make her not care and my mom hung up on her. Her office was small so when she called my parents, she had the phone on speaker. I do not understand the 100 yards situation I just know my mom didn't want to have anything to do with me. The intake lady who was helping me claimed she never had a case where a juvenile had turned themselves in as a ward of the state. I was only tired of going from house to house and the anxiety of not knowing where I was going to sleep. Tired of walking the streets all night wandering like a little lost puppy. I was about to have a baby soon I had to find somewhere to go, and this had to be better than wandering around all night. She contacted a couple of agencies some I was too old for.

Others were not taking in teens that were pregnant, the first place they sent me was to a group home. The group home was in a secure location hidden in a court in a place called Edge moor which is right outside of Wilmington. The group home was ok for the most part everyone in there was younger than me. Since I was a teenager, I was allowed to cook and assist the workers. I

Over the weekend I was given a weekend pass and allotted some time to go spend some time with my dad and family. When I returned to the group home someone had stolen my shoes.

I could not find them, and I searched everyone's rooms with or without permission. I was livid and I packed my shit and left went back to see the lady at the courthouse. She ended up putting me in a group home on the west side. It was ok except these parents paid attention and we had rules. We had to be in at certain times and do chores and we were disciplined if our tasks were incomplete. I ended up breaking curfew one too many times and well I was not allowed to come back to the group home.

Next step we decided to do foster care and give me to a foster parent which was a little better than a group home where everybody's belongings were accessible to everyone.

I was put in foster care and sent to the Northside to go live with my foster mother a single black lady. I hoped this would be a good fit as I was getting tired of packing my clothes up all the time. It was a little weird at first, but I began to fit in cause the other foster kids were girls my age. They easily hipped me to the house rules what we could and could not get away with. My foster mother did have one child there that belonged to her. She was an adult just do not remember her age and she was handicapped as she could not speak, she was deaf. The problem that I did not have a bed to sleep in at night was fixed.

I did however have to pay attention to my personal items and clothes as I was being stolen from on the regular. That is the big problem with group homes and foster homes. People did not respect personal spaces and property and my foster mom did not care. She just wanted the check we could have done anything we wanted she just gave us a place to rest our heads. Me being the person I am hated being there.

I dealt with it as much as I could until I could not do it anymore then I began to make plans to move again. It was now almost winter, so it was chilly outside almost Halloween in the city. The night before Halloween was considered mischief night when teens would just trash the city, houses, and people's cars. We woke up on Halloween and our house and the neighbors had been tissu-ed. We opened the front door that morning to a web of toilet paper everywhere. My foster mom was so upset we thought it was so funny.

I thought it was great maybe she could clean it up and do something with her time. For the most part, being in a foster home was ok still, I pretended, acting as if everything was ok. I really missed my kid!

One day I called to talk to my daughter and me and my mom talked for a bit. She told me she missed me and now and then someone comes to her house unexpectedly and she would hope it was me. Unfortunately, I was 4 hours away so that was not happening.

I was a little stressed as me and my baby's dad were not together, we actually weren't on speaking terms. He felt as if I wasn't pregnant, and he was too busy juggling other girls and his baby's moms. Even though there were always people around I was so lonely. Everyone who really knew me was so extremely far and I was tired of being introduced all the time to different people. I felt like I was always tensed or anxious all the time.

Longing to be near my loved ones and trying to figure out how I could fix this problem so I could get my other baby. Well, she was not a baby anymore I had missed a birthday she was almost 2. How could I have been having another baby and was not even a mom to my first baby? Determined as I was to fix this, I was on a mission to get to VA.

I begin to reach out to my friends that I was close to. Me and 5-6 other girls I felt close to like actual friends that I left behind in Va. Me and one of my friends kept in contact and I mentioned to her that I wanted to come back. The only problem was I did not have anywhere to live. Figured if I could show my mom I was back and that I was taking care of me she might love me. Not so sure why her opinion mattered so much to me I just wanted her to be happy with me,

love me maybe and be proud of me.

One of the hardest life lessons was trying to get my mother's love. I was doing magic tricks trying to get her to see me believe in me. Why did she always think so negatively towards me?

Just wanted her to see I was not all bad, just needed someone anyone to support me. I understand that my mom was her own person she had grown up in an abusive home. Not a lot of details were talked about I just knew that she had come from abuse. My mom probably had me before she even begins to heal her own self. Never will I go into detail about my mom without her permission as I don't want to trigger anything. My mom has been through a lot and I don't understand her triggers. I genuinely care for her and I know like me she was a kid going thru a lot of these situations. All these hoops I was jumping through didn't matter she was never paying attention.

Like me, she probably thought she would take her family and move far away from toxic people and situations. She was also a young girl faced with adult situations. When you become an adult, you try to heal and live as if life is normal. Trying to learn yourself is remarkably interesting and not so easy when you add children and a spouse to the mix. Did I remind her of the pain? Who knows I could, she was way too prideful to ever admit that she was mistreating me? Deep down I know she was battling her own demons.

As a child, I didn't understand the situation was painful probably for us both. I felt we were in a better place because of our last conversation. If I can get to VA without my mom knowing and pop up on her I could make her so happy. After all, she did tell me she wished I were knocking on the door and was the surprise. I could make that dream come true for us.

My girlfriend ended talking to her grandmother who allowed homeless people a place to stay. She never had any children it was mostly grown people, but she let me come anyway. My homegirl came thru for me and convinced her grandmother to let me stay. Now all I had to do was come up with the money to catch the bus and I would be on my way. In the weeks to come, I didn't get upset with anything that was going on I knew before long I would be in VA. My daughter would be in my arms and I would really be able to smile again. When I tell you, I felt great I thought things were going in the right direction soon I was on my way.

I got to Virginia, in early December 1992. When I got to VA, I had someone come pick me up from the bus station and I needed them to do one thing. I needed to go past my mom's house and surprise her as I promised myself I would. When I got to my mom's house, I was so excited. Dam near tripped walking up the steps my big pregnant self in December. Immediately I began to knock on the door with my finger over the peephole so no one could see who it was.

One of my siblings asked who it is I could hear my daughter in the background making noises. I didn't say one-word at all, boy was I about to give them the surprise of their life.

Because I did not answer the question my mom came to the door and was like who it is. Still not answering she opened the door and I said Surprise and reached in to hug her.

She didn't reciprocate my embrace rather she asked why I came to her house unannounced. I said remember our phone call when you told me you wished one day you would open the door and it was me. I

just wanted to surprise you. She said do not come to my house again unannounced. My heart dropped are you kidding. I moved back I found myself a place to stay she didn't seem to be interested in what I was saying. My brother and sister were in the background excited to see me.

I could not even speak to them we were all suffering. This is horrible my daughter was in the back of my mom crawling towards the door. I asked if I could hug her, she told me to call and she would allow me to visit. So again, broken-hearted I walked away unable to touch my child. I was distraught yet hopeful.

My daughter started crying she knew who I was but did not understand my distance towards her. During this time in my life, I learned too not to be too comfortable. Did not matter to me if it was people, places, or things. From this point me being comfortable was a wrap, to me was for the weak. I became very insecure, troubled, couldn't relax at all everything was perceived as a threat. My safety was always at risk to me. You know when a person senses a potentially threatening situation. Their body does this flight or fight response thing when you may have systems of like rapid heartbeat, shallow breathing muscle tenseness.

All are common during fight or flight, right? I lived that way daily. My actions were all like calculated steps to make sure, I was safe. Everything and everyone around me annoyed me I was always so uptight, could never just be myself. Protection mode was where I found myself all the time. Like a momma bear with her bear cub, I overly had my back. You might think you were close; it was a game. Sort of anyways the closer you think you are the farther you really are. My heart was aching from being too comfortable, not being on guard, people that were around I felt I could not trust.

Everyone I let in had hurt me that was the first thing I worked on not letting or allowing anyone in. Such a pretty face so many problems. I became very guarded towards the world as a whole; my guard was constantly up because I felt no reciprocity from others. I could just shut people out with no regard. The walls I put up were high and thick like vault doors I would rather be closed off from the world than be in everyone's face. I had; had my share of people.

Being homeless even though nobody knew, taught me a lot.

People are more fake than real, like some kind of dis-ease. When I am in control, I am safe. When others are in control it's suspect, outside of me I don't know who got me. People would do anything to look good in the eyes of another. They had pretty faces but they were full of deceit. So full of love and innocence trusting the wrong people hurt me. The faces that I investigated I couldn't even trust.

Finally, I was back in VA. When I got dropped off at my friends' grandmothers, I dried my face up and walked into the house. My friend was in there with her mom waiting on my arrival. They wanted to make sure our meet and greet was comfortable.

My homegirl's grandma was old school and when my friend left, she begins to question me. What did you do to get kicked out she wanted to know?

Well as you can imagine with my talkative self, I told her everything. She listened asked questions and make comments. She indeed was a grandma and told me the rules to the house, my curfew, where my bedroom was, and who all lived in the home. She said she was tired had to be up early and was going to bed.

I had a boyfriend that I was dating at the time.

No, he was he was not the father of my baby. He was actually the same guy I dated before I left to go to Delaware. Met him at a church event my mom took us to when I was pregnant with my first daughter. We had met and became friends right before my oldest daughter was to be born. He was attracted to me and wanted to date me, but

I had way too much going on. However, we developed a friendship that had lasted almost 2 years now.

He had anger issues and was very argumentative we always argued because he felt he was a professor.

Always trying to teach me what he learned.

When my mom kicked me out, he snuck me into his home returning the favor I had given him. He and his mom were having problems one day and I snuck him into my house.

So, he didn't have to sleep outside. So yes, they let me stay until my dad got my ticket to come to him. His mom didn't like me she thought I was fast, and I was going to end up pregnant with his baby. Now once I had moved to Delaware our relationship was over. At least I thought so anyway. He constantly reminded me that I cheated.

Was he crazy, I lived 4 hours away? The only way I am going to be faithful to you is if I am with you, daily. We talked a lot on the phone when I left Va. I mean what more could we actually do. My dad was like all these dudes in this city and you saving yourself for him. We laughed so much about that. That was another cool thing about being raised by a man.

Daddy knew men and he had swag he was classy and had so much game.

He taught me and my sister about men. We watched him juggle multiple women with finesse. Boy did we have questions we had many conversations with him about these topics? He just answered our questions, for the most part, we might have listened. Just thinking about this is so amusing. Either way, this dude that I had connected to once I got back to my little town was not good for me. He and I had a very toxic relationship as kids, but I thought it was love. It was almost the exact relationship I had with my mom. He just was not my parent, but a person I was interested in dating.

The dude I was messing with had control issues not even understanding what any of that meant at the time, I dated this young man. The cycles were starting in my life they had begun, and I was ignorant and clueless to what was happing around me.

One dreary night while I was hanging out with him, he got terribly angry with me. Suddenly, he just started fighting me out of nowhere. What the heck is the problem why was he so freaking angry. We are arguing about something none of us can control at this point Yes, I am pregnant and no you are not the father.

Of course, I know this I am the one who actually had sex to get this way. If I thought I would be back in Va. I probably could have stayed faithful. His argument was nonsense, well I mean now that I think about it. I am not so sure I could not understand what his problem was as I was trying to survive my harsh life. He was furious that I was pregnant, and the baby was not his. We were underage he knew that I couldn't control the situation, but I guess he wanted me to think that he was hopelessly waiting on my return to Va. Just a whole lot of arguing and wasting time if you asked me. you cared that my baby belonged to someone else. This had to be the stupidest argument in America I thought. Yeah, he wanted me to feel bad that I had a baby that was not his.

How I saw It was we can always make another baby, Sir. I was not about to feel any kind of way about myself, personally, I had other more pressing shit to deal with.

Dude I have not seen you in a whole two years like really. Either way, he did not want me near and would get mad when I walked away so we fought. Confusing right yeah, I know, my butt was attracted to that crazy mess.

NO GOOD! Unknown to me a guy was looking at us from afar off came and rushed over. He grabbed my then-boyfriend, yoked him up. We were in downtown Portsmouth which was different from where I grew up in Cavalier Manor.

So, this area was considered downtown not so sure the section of town. Would not want to even say the wrong section as these people rep these neighborhoods and to some, it is considered disrespect. However, there were more random people on the street and this dude appeared out of nowhere. He scared the crap out of me and dude.

He said, "I know I didn't see you fighting on this woman."

"She pregnant, are you crazy?" he asked.

The dude told me to leave so I did. He told me that I had no business being with any many that felt ok with putting his hands on me. I got out of there and went home. When I got in Mrs. Grandma was like, "You ok?" "Yes, ma'am," I replied. She was like, "Why you are breathing so hard." Was I breathing hard? Well, I could have been boy was she good. She was such a sweet little lady you couldn't put anything past her.

She stood shorter than me. That did not mean anything she had a mouth like she was 6feet. They did not mess with her either, she was feisty. "Seems like you were running or fighting for your life." She said walking away. I just looked at her how could she know? Then again, she was a grandma, felt like my grandmother.

Think if I got out of line, she might have even popped me.

GOT TO GETAWAY

What I did not know was the guy who rescued me was my home-girl's uncle. So, he had told Ms. Grandma that some dude who was supposed to be my boyfriend was fighting with me. She went in on me, she had been watching me she stated. In the passing weeks, she felt I was misguided and unsupported. She went on to say that I would probably end up having to take my mom to court for custody of my daughter.

"I know you might not want to go down that route, but I do not think your mom is going to just give her to you." She spoke. "Do you want your other daughter?" she asked. "If so, you must come up with a plan because you're pregnant again?"

She was so sweet, and she helped me look at things from a different perspective. She and every woman in my life that sowed into me had different views. They all would tell me it is going to be rough, but I could make it.

My cousins found out I was in town. Well, she wasn't really my cousin but someone who went to church with and knew since I live in VA. She heard I was in town and pregnant and told me I could come live with her. She would not charge me any rent until after I had my baby. The reason she said this was to allow me to get myself together, she told me she would help me get a job after the baby and that then I could begin to pay rent. I thought that would be a cool idea.

How would I tell Mrs. Grandma she was very mothering and genuinely seemed to care about my well-being? For a girl aged 17, she felt that I had moved way too many times and I needed more stability and structure in my life. When I mentioned it to her, she said, "It's your choice, baby." She was upset with those in charge of my well-being she felt that they just pushed me off on everyone else she told me she was bothered that it took this long for anyone to want me. She knew that my mom and some family members were there in Va.

She felt like a dog was being treated better than I was. Ms. Grandma was definitely old school, and she felt my mom was acting recklessly. She told me she would pray for me and that God would give me wisdom for some direction she just did not understand why my family did not seem to care about what happened to me.

As 1992 was ending we were getting ready for the holidays. I decided to take my cousin/friend up on her offer. I moved in with her right before the holiday season. Christmas was right around the corner I had received a call that my granddad was sick. I remember going up to the hospital I hitched a ride up there and met my aunts and some other family. We had not seen each other in so long as they all moved from the part of Va. Everyone was sad losing a parent for anyone is never a good thing. My aunts were always genuinely concerned about Ray Ray.

After visiting my grandfather, me and my auntie sat in the car and talked for hours, we talked about me and my mom and just where I was going in life. She told me some things I needed to hear some things I did not want to hear. She was another person that I could be around without faking. That night we did not know what was going to happen with my granddad.

The Christmas holiday was days away when I received the news that my grandpa had died. I was supposed to attend my grandfather's funeral, but I didn't. My mom told me she would pick me up for the funeral, just to call me while I was waiting to tell me that she was not able to come to get me. Her excuse was it was out of the way. So, she didn't come here to get me, unfortunately, I never got to say goodbye and I loved my granddad he; he took up for me a lot. Don't really think he cared too much for my mom. I remember he took up for me against my mom, meant a lot to me plus he was the only grandad that I knew until I was 16.

R.I.P. Grandpa M. Williams. My oldest son has your first name, it's his middle name. Thanks so much for the time we had to spend together.

I still was unable to see my child even though I was in the same state not even a full 30minutes away well maybe but still.

My friend that I was now staying with knew my mom. She knew that I was not really allowed to see my daughter she understood the history I and my mom had. We all had gone to church together and sang in the choir. These were the only people my mom trusted me to be around and that is what it's funny.

We partied; I mean who does not, but we partied. We never got caught and we had some very memorable moments. Like I said we had known each other since I was young. It was just me and my siblings growing up in VA so they would be considered like big cousins. Dang, just could not seem to get that sentence out.

We talked about it and she promised that she would get my daughter to be able to have visits to see me. Man, that would make me so happy. I do not know about any other parent. It was hard for me to be in the same city with my kid and not see her. She was a part of me, and I needed to know she was ok she was my responsibility. Yes, I do appreciate my mom stepping in to help. What I didn't appreciate was her using her authority to manipulate the situation, nor did I appreciate her controlling ways.

Being unable to see my child was indeed hard that was just excessively mean to me, period, however, she came thru as well. Before I knew it, my friend had convinced my mom to allow my daughter to spend some time alone with me at her home. My daughter was coming over and staying all day sometimes and occasionally, she might even stay the night yasssss. I simply was so overly excited with this news; I was delighted all I could think of is that my children would at least be able to have a relationship with each other.

Guess I was worried about the sibling, sister bond. Me and my siblings had fun growing up, we played pranks, we made fun out of everything.

Like I said my mom and stepdad were not rich, but we were far from poor. We could just look at each other and laugh at the craziest of things guess I wanted my children to have that same bond. Naturally, I hoped for the best, I did not know how to get past those feelings just didn't want my children to be strangers. Dang, this was so messy man, it never had to be this complicated.

What seemed like forever was how things were moving.

I would get frustrated, but I stayed patient and humbled myself for the greater good. Being at my friend's house was fun as hell. We would have parties on the weekend and all the sleepovers and pranks you could ask for. Man, we would have so much fun but there were some very crazy moments as well. Life is real you know good and bad are always present.

I started dating a guy that would come over to the gatherings we would have. He knew I was pregnant at this point it was obvious that I had a bundle coming soon. One day he asked me what was going on with the baby's dad and what did I have for my baby. So, I explained to him the story behind me and my daughter's dad. Didn't really have too many things for my baby I really had not obtained any job and didn't anticipate getting one anytime soon with this growing belly.

Well at this point I could have been a risk for most jobs.

Or they figured as soon as they hired me, I was going to need maternity leave.

People were giving me things not sure if it was a girl or a boy I had little universal baby garments. He just listened to my story and we talked some more before he left for the night. The next day he called to see what I was doing if I wanted to hang out.

Sure, come on, what am I doing anyway? He picked me up and took me out to eat which was so fun. I can't say I had been taken out on a date my whole pregnancy. When we left, he drove to a department store and we went in we walked to the baby section and he started picking out baby items.

He was like, "You need this."

Or he might say "This would be great for either sex, right?"

"What are you doing, why are we over here."

"You need some baby stuff the baby about to be here in a week."

We both laughed.

"You know the baby not going to be here in a week."

"But you need some stuff, get what you need."

"Seriously?" I asked

"Do not get too excited." He said smiling from ear to ear. He was a mess I tell you. "Thank you so much you are the best," I replied hugging his neck. He spent money on some nice items for my baby. Now I didn't have to worry she/he would come into the world with gifts. Plus, people you know how we do pass things down that are in great condition to the next mother. cause baby anything is high everyday all day. I was in the game he blessed the hell out of me. I was stunned that he like me enough to spend money on me and my baby aww,

I felt blessed he was a great friend.

One of the nicest gestures a man ever did for me unexpectedly. Now I was ready for the baby and well, looked like we went shopping just in time cause my baby was almost here. Over the next couple of weeks, I and my friends would prepare the room and get it ready for the baby.

One of my other friends was in the room talking to me one day about my plans.

She was trying to figure out what my plans were once my baby got here. She was a sister to the friend I lived with. She warned me to be careful and not trust anyone as if maybe, I might have been getting too comfortable. Well, that's how I saw it, so you know I go into crazy panic mode and just start thinking about my next move.

She told me that she knew I was being promised one thing.

That I was also being told another. They were talking about me behind closed doors basically, she cared, and she did not want me to be misled. Traps were being prepared for me that I needed to look out for she did not want me to fall for them.

She was being told that once March came, I had to leave the residence and find my own way. Amongst other things, none of which was ever told to me. It was all good though cause maybe I was acting comfortably.

Even though I work so hard at not being comfortable. Thank you for that information and from that point on I acted as if I was told I had to go, period. I begin to wonder with my baby due in at least the next 2 months, where were we going to go. My baby was born a little late 42-week-long pregnancy was what I had endured and now finally, it came to an end. March 93, my second daughter was born. Usually, when a baby is born late, they say it is due to stress but that was not the case with me.

Unless the doctor's dates could have been off by 2 weeks.

Once my baby was born, it was time to get busy working on my next move. Of course, my body must heal from delivery, but I didn't have 6 weeks to rest. My mom called me one day and told me that my god sister in California was looking for me she wanted to see how I was doing. When I called her, she told me that she had been asking for me, but my mom wouldn't give her any information.

She had informed me that my mom told her I needed to be worried about where I was going to live. Mommy had told her that I was being put out, what I did not understand is why not tell me if that was indeed how the person felt. However, I can't control anyone's actions but my own.

If it wasn't for me speaking to my other friend I would have been totally in the dark, I hadn't even heard that much. Why this was so crazy was because were lived in the same house and had plenty of conversations every day so why not tell me that you don't want me in the house didn't that make way more sense. Unless of course this was all a façade and she was being fake, she did tell me some similar things to my friend's sister's story, boy for her to be all the way in California she was dead on. Wow, I just did not understand why people were not straightforward with how they felt. I blamed no one it had begun to be normal for me to last in a place 3-6 months. My god-sister did not like the girl I was staying with because she knew that information was being held from me. The way she explained it the girl and my mom were working together.

Had she only allowed me to stay to make it seem as if she cared, was she reporting stuff to my mom about conversations we had about matters of my heart? Playing both sides of the fence was something I hated that people did, I felt like I was being manipulated again, trust was so hard for me to have. It was easier for me to see people as enemies rather than friends at this point. So, when my god-sister suggested that I come to Cali, I felt that was the best plan.

My god-sister had moved away, and nobody knew what she was doing with her life. Not having any other ideas, I allowed her to pay my way to California.

She offered to get me a plane ticket. My baby was not even a month yet, I do not think she was even 2 weeks before I left. Oh well, west coast here we come, just not by air I was so scared to fly, we argued for a whole week about the journey. There was no way I was going to fly, scared to death, she laughed so hard. How can I hold a newborn and get on a plane and not panic? I didn't see any other way, the bus it was going to be.

If I took the bus it would take 3 days, I was simply fine with that. My friend never got the chance to put me out I also never told her that I knew she was putting me out. With the help of my god sister by the time she found out my ticket was purchased. She told me that she didn't want me to go especially with the baby being so young. At that point I knew she was not sincere, so it really did not matter, I had to go.

She told me she was sad that I hadn't confided in her to let her know I was leaving. Because I am genuinely not fake it's hard to flat out lie to people. Now my feelings were something that might have been fake, that was truly how I was surviving, so I will not stop now. Sometimes things are meant to be said other times it's simply better to let things be as they are.

So, when she was talking, and I didn't know what to said I just became quiet.

Could not tell her that I had no plans of ever seeing her again in life because I didn't. I can honestly say to this day if I ever did see her again it was very brief cause I still can't remember when the last time I ever saw that lady again.

Time to move on to the next chapter of my life. I had to go I had overstayed my welcome. If you aren't for me, you must be against me you know? Not a problem at all, act as if they all are against you and push forward thoughts of a 17-year-old in America.

Another adventure was waiting for me to come aboard I got on the greyhound me and my baby with $20 for food. The trip was going to take 3 whole days a bit longer than the plane but a lot less anxiety. My god-sister tried to get my mom to give me some traveling money for my trip. At that point in my life, I think my mom would have rather heard I was dead than find a way to help me. Back in 1993, it was a bit harder to send money.

We didn't have Zelle or Cash app available I'm quite sure Western Union was probably the way money was being sent or mail. So funny how times have totally changed. Whether I had money or not wasn't what I was worried about. Getting out of a house where I was not wanted was way more important to me. How could I go forward if everything was pulling me backward? Here I was again, leaving my daughter behind.

She was able to meet her little sister whom I told her was her baby, she didn't understand but she loved the baby. For me in my little mind seemed like I just could not get a break. The last time I saw my daughter before I left, we talked. Yep, she was little didn't understand anything that I probably was saying to her. I still talked to her told her I loved her and me and the baby were going away, assuring her that we would be back for her. Begging her to not forget her sister or her mother promising her we would not forget her.

You not going to see me for a while, but I will call and talk to you every chance I get. So sorry that I must leave you again. If I had waited until I was a grown lady, we would not be faced with such problems.

That is not the reality I wanted for my little family, but it was the reality I was dealing with. I love you beautiful we all hugged each other tight, my beautiful little girl. I wanted her to feel as loved as a person could feel always happy, with constant smiles on her face daily. Living her best life as best as I could provide. Goodbyes were always so hard for me as I suffer from separation attachment issues. I hate to leave, and it causes more anxieties.

I just believed that God would provide a way. Whatever was higher than I knew that I loved this kid and wanted to do the right thing.

The universe at least had to have my back.

CALI

The trip to California was long but very adventurous. It took three whole days to get there, but do you know how much I was able to see because I took that long trip? Oh, this was the furthest I had ever been traveling in my entire life. Buses stop everywhere, I did not have to worry about feeding my daughter because I breastfed her.

The money I had was enough to get me some food, I just had to stretch it, now that would have been hard today but 26 years ago things were different.

I remember going down from VA to points south. Before this trip, the furthest south I had ever been, was North Carolina for church events with my mom. This bus went to every state from Louisiana to Texas. So many different views to see mom and pop stores and little country shops with millions of souvenirs. The state of Texas to me was huge it took 24 hours to get out of that state. It was dry flat land and hot, boy was it hot. Most residents in the tidewater area of VA either liked the redskins or the Dallas Cowboys.

We rode right past the home of the Dallas Cowboys.

The stadium was located in Erving, Texas. How cool to be able to see something in person that you could only see on television. It begins to get dark in Texas but over on the horizon I could see that it was still day in California. Such a pretty sight to be able to see day and night at the same time. We still were far from Los Angeles which was my destination.

When we got close to California some of the people had been watching me from other states, but I did not know anyone was paying me attention. I remember we stopped to get something to eat, and I did not get off the bus. Some of the riders bought me and my baby food she could not eat it, but they saw everyone eating except me and got me something to eat for me.

After I ate my food someone tapped me on my shoulder, wow we had finally made it to the great state of California.

When I turned around to see who was tapping me. A brown hair gentleman says, "Hey we wanted you to have this." He handed me about $55 in cash. "We collected this because we care, we Californians take care of each other." He said.

Everyone on the bus including the bus driver had blessed me. I do not even know if I can describe in words how that made me feel. I swear it's just the little things that may my heart so happy. When I feel nobody cares someone always changes my mind.

No one in the world I knew would give me money, but these strangers found it in their heart too, that touched my soul I was so in awe that they really came together for little ole me. I ended up telling them that I was going to stay with my godsister, and I had never been to Cali. They told me they had watched me not get off the bus at any stop to feed me or the baby.

So, a couple of them went to the other passengers and ask them to donate to help feed us.

I explained I was breastfeeding, and they felt I needed extra nutrients so now I could purchase what I needed. Amazing people promise I cannot make these stories up.

California was so beautiful; I remember going thru Palm Springs such a different world from VA or Delaware. They had mountains with ice on the top because they were so high in the air how cool was that. It was as if I was back at Manor High or Glasgow in Geography class. I loved to travel and be able to see beautiful places around the world. There is one of my aunts and a

cousin I have that's always traveling and I am always asking to be part of somebody's luggage. They travel and go everywhere, one day I am going to, I was told to get a Passport.

You do not have to tell me twice. Every city was different from the next city that we traveled to I was so happy to be in California. The architectural structures were so freaking cool!

So much to see everywhere people live so many various lifestyles so intriguing. The country was the country to the bone desolate as hell.

The cities were different, one may say they are from the city, but I did not really agree. Some cities were like country cities a couple of buildings nothing spectacular to look at. Maybe some cool diners decorated to draw one's attention. I consider cities to be like New York, Philadelphia, Wilmington which is tiny as heck. These are what I consider a city Places like Tampa I consider in the middle somewhere; I call that a country city. Mostly because it is a city, not row houses, but things are convenient, and I do not have to have a car to get around. If I must have a car, we in the country.

Period totally just how you feel.

Currently, I had never been to LA did not know what I was in store for. When we were pulling into the bus stations. I saw buildings houses made from stucco I believe, graffiti about as much as New York even though it was spacey to me. The cars had hydraulics in almost every other car. How cool was that? The more we approached the bus station I saw what appeared to be pimps and prostitutes. Oh, my but they didn't look like any prostitute's id ever seen. Never seen a real-life pimp, they were clean. I mean pinstripe suits, gators all I can think of is Pinky and Kat Williams on Friday, hair fried and under a hat.

These girls were beautiful, and their garments man are they prostitutes for real? These ladies had on apparel that looked like it was as much as a rent payment. They look good who would not want to be with them. This was not the type of prostitute I was used to seeing. Do not judge me, I am so serious right now.

I thought this place was about to be very intriguing. If they were on drugs, they hid it quite well they were sharply dressed their rags were nice, in my Cooley High voice. Boy was I excited my god sister met me at the bus station with her and her husband. Lol, they critiqued my clothing because there are a lot of gangs in LA. I had on a lot of blues and they did not want me to be approached by the Blood gang. We drove all thru LA this place was nice and indeed a city. Different architectural structures altogether but really unique. The trees were tall so tall in this state. There were restaurants I had never heard of in my life. There were indeed gangs Bloods and Crips territories had graffiti all over everything.

They explained to me that I had to pay attention they would carjack people at the lights. You had to not let them catch you slipping. It was classy in Long Beach to me Compton looked like you really do not want to be there unless you had to. I had to go to get me a replacement id while I was there, looked aggressive to me. I was on Pacific Coast Highways a main strip in the city it was so nice with many comedy clubs all over. My god-sister lived in Seal Beach on military housing. Her husband was stationed in Long Beach and it was really nice there.

I could walk to the beach right from her house, everything comes with a price in life. I was learning so many valuable lessons. Me and my god sister got along great I was learning not to get too close, didn't matter who they were and what our relationship was about no matter who

they were just never wanted to get so close anymore.

When we first got to her house, they took apart my suitcase I couldn't wear anything but my jeans.

I had a lot of blue and because of gang

violence was so real in this area clothing could make or break you. I had to were neutral colors. Not too much blue or red together or yellow. Yep, you guessed we went shopping because I was not going to be limited to just 1 or 2 outfits. There was so much I needed to see but I was not trying to date. Being focused was important to me and I felt that guys were distractions, and I did not have time for the drama right now.

Did not know what triggered people, but I tried to learn them to avoid problems. Probably some people-pleasing stuff was there too, oh well. To me it was survival, and I did not have just me to think about anymore. I needed to get stable so I could get my oldest child back my daughters needed to play with each other and share secrets. Support each other's dreams and goals and get into arguments and find ways to be angry at me. Sisters were amazing they could admire you and get jealous over little to nothing. I had to get a grip and find a way to turn things around for the better. Either way, I could have stayed in Cali for a while, but I just stayed for like 3 months.

It was great amazing weather and chilly nights with no clouds. I went to the Soul Train building and I saw where all the people go for rehearsals or auditions. My god sister also took me to Hollywood oh my. Such a lavish elegant looking place, the street signs are what did it for me. There is also a massive amount of homeless people in California. I cannot remember the name of the place we went to, but it was so many homeless people! Looked like a whole other cityscape. The music was different also in California. Being from the northeast in Delaware we had good music.

Not saying the West coast did not have good music I just didn't know any other artist other than the Dre, Snoop, and old groups from back in the day.

I think they just play more west coast artist music over there and vice versa.

It was great they have some amazing food places over there. I had the time of my life it was a different vibe but cool as hell and I loved it. My sister contacted me, she was pregnant and about to have my first nephew in Delaware. Not only that, but I also received a call that my little cousin had got shot and killed.

My friends play too much, so I did not want to hear that and frankly, I didn't believe it. If indeed, this was true why had not my sister told me? I did not believe it but oh how sad, sad, sad the thought of death made me feel. Even if it was not true the city can be so mean and cold person to person. I needed to get back home because well dad and the family missed me.

My daughters' father was also pestering me.

For someone so certain this baby wasn't his he was sure mad that he had not seen her and that I had traveled all the way to California with her before I came up north. More than that he was angry at me, because well I didn't give her his last name. "She must not be my baby."

He whined. Nah I just felt like she is a Williams for sure. So, she not getting your last name you rejected me soon as you found out I was pregnant.

We were kids he was doing what was best for him like college and I was doing what was best for me and the baby we created. We had not even spoken my whole pregnancy, he left just like everyone else. What I wasn't going to do was beg him to stay, so we went separate ways.

I got a ticket back home from a dude in the military that my god sister introduced me to. Unfortunately, it was about time to say goodbye for now to sunny California.

I had a great time from the time I got to California until I left.

They wanted me to come back to life. That was a commitment that I just could not make.

Of course, I was not being put out or sent away, my godsister was godsent. I had so much fun and such an amazing time. However, I greatly missed my family and was ready to see them. Before I left, I promised my god sister I would not give up on me or my situation.

I would get my daughter back if that were the last thing on Earth I did.

She gave me a huge hug as she dropped me off at the bus station on my way to Philly.

During my trip back home, things got a little hectic. I remember on the way back there was a layover I believe, in the state of New Mexico.

Well, when you are boarding the bus you must get in line at a specific time and go through the gate. You must stand in line to hold your spot so they can get a headcount. I was standing in line just me and my baby when the lady that was in front of me was being a little annoying, I was not really paying her attention. She just

acted irritated as if she were bothered by me or the people in front of her.

Man, people are weird who would have known unless she verbalized what she felt.

Anyway, I took a step back just because I know me and my personal space issues.

Well, my baby's pacifier fell out of her mouth I had to bend over to get it off the ground. The lady turned around and made a face of disapproval.

I was like "What is good."

She was like, "I am tired of your baby touching me."

Listen, I swear I can't make this shit up. My baby had just turned 3months she was not actually touching anyone. So, I was like "Ma'am!" She appeared to be an older white lady. Not grandma old she just looked old. "My baby did not touch you I don't know what you got going on. Your problem isn't with my baby or me," I told her So, others in the line noticed that the lady just appeared to be having weird reactions to everyone. I cannot really explain but we all had to deal with this crazy lady.

Not judging just saying. So now it's time to get on the bus we are all walking in line and the bus driver is checking tickets. The lady begins to argue with the bus driver about something that had nothing to do with anything. Everyone was just looking around maybe she was mental she was straight tripping, either way. I thought it was just in the way. She got on the bus and I was now stepping on the bus me and my baby begin to walk on the bus. When I got right beside the bus drivers' seat, she turned around to me.

She was like, "I am tired of your baby hitting me in my head." The one Spanish lady looked at me and said, "Give me your baby!"

I don't know if she saw the look in my eyes, but before the lady could hit me, I had hit her and well we were fighting on the Greyhound bus.

I was 17 years old in New Mexico a place I knew no one. My god sister was far away in Cali. The bus driver broke up the fight and was angered at our actions. He was like what is wrong with you guys, I tried to explain but he told us we had to get off his bus and could not ride. The lady handed me my baby and security had made us go back inside of the terminal. I was livid how the hell, matter of fact how the hell did this all just go down like that. Who was this woman she had to be psycho; my baby could not even reach that far?

I just began to cry, and I put a couple of dollars in the payphone so I could call my god sister as I watched the bus back out of the terminal. Man, this was a messy situation. When my god sister answered the phone, I begin to explain to her what had just happened.

While talking to her I see someone running towards me gesturing for me to come here. It was the bus driver who had kicked me off the bus moments ago.

He said, "Hurry up let's go", so I ran. Man, when I tell you I ran on the bus the whole bus started clapping. With tears in my eyes, I promise I did not understand what was going on. The bus driver got on the microphone and was like.

"I want to apologize for kicking you off the bus". He said "All the passengers on the bus begin to attack him and fuss with him, demanding that he return to the terminal and pick me up because all you had done was defend yourself. I promise yaw all my life I just been trying to defend myself and prove how I am ok.

These were strangers I do not remember one name or have any telephone numbers to have to agree with my story. This did happen to me, that was miraculous. The whole trip to California was absolutely amazing, wish it were closer to home. Nah Cali is a vibe I will most def be back. If I had it my way I would drive back out there.

I love the view goodbye Cali I love You!

BACK AND FORTH

When I arrived in Philadelphia, my sister was there big and pregnant with my nephew. She and my cousin were there to greet me. My cousin and sister drove to Philly to come to get me, from Delaware. While in California I had received a call that one of my cousins had been killed. My sister had been ordered by my aunt to bring me to her house so that she could help me deal with the loss.

The very first house we stopped at was my aunt's house, to find out if the information was true. Indeed, he had been shot and killed on the bridge one night on his way home after enjoying a great night with friends. I was just heartbroken; I was never able to tell him goodbye. Who would just open fire and kill someone, just heartless acts of violence? He had an ongoing case that my aunt had to attend so that a conviction would be made. She informed me that the sentencing was coming, and I could attend to help me with closure.

This time around being in Delaware wasn't so bad. I had made friends, developed relationships with people who knew I was without parental guidance. Some people loved my dad so much that because I was his child, their love just poured over onto me. While I did not have a specific place to call home, I did have a few places that I and my daughter could crash. There were people in Delaware that did genuinely love me and would never put me out because of respect for my dad and family name.

My daughter's dad at the time was in college, attending Del State. Once he found out that I was back in town he stated he would be coming up from Dover for the weekend. He wanted to meet his baby finally as now she was at least 4 months old. He was extremely excited to meet her, but a little doubtful, he had two sons so he thought all he could make were boys. Well jokes on him because we made a girl and she looked just like him. Why I didn't give her his last name was something we argued about for many years to come.

Not my fault if he wanted her name to be his I felt he would have been around to make sure that happened. Be mad at yourself, not me, we were young and dumb. Plus, he was cheating on me the entire relationship, so he wasn't a factor anymore. We just had a child, so we had to deal with each other I tried to respect his wishes if I could, but we did not even really know each other.

We met at McDonald's while I was working the year before.

He thought I was pretty and wanted to take me out on a date. He and his friend competed as to who would date me.

He was a little shorter than most guys I dated but I gave him a chance. He had a little swag about him. After dating for about two weeks, he asked if I wanted to move in with him. Didn't really pay him too much attention as I figured he was not serious. Since I was living everywhere and he wanted out of his mom's house, it might work. After a couple of dates, he asked again, if I wanted to move in with him and some roommates.

His brother had met a girl that had a place she couldn't afford so since we had jobs, they thought it would be a good idea. Since it was four of us, we split the rent four ways and it was not too much for any of us.

I probably wasn't allowed to move in with my boyfriend, but It was cool with me.

We had our own place for about 2 months, long enough to get pregnant. For whatever reason, we ended up losing our place. The girl who stayed there with the brother's girlfriend

was so behind in rent our little money wasn't helping anything. My daughter's dad moved back home and moved me in at least until his mom caught us.

He had a football scholarship so regardless I was about to be back homeless soon. We tried but it did not work.

Needless to say, he ended up having to go back to college, so we were not on the same path. Meanwhile, I was in a good place at that time. I had two aunts within walking distance of each other on the west side. One lived down the hill the other lived across the bridge. I would juggle houses from my aunts to my dad's girlfriend that lived on the hill. Having my second child helped me a great deal, having another child out of wedlock was probably not great and the fact I did not have a diploma or anything looked terribly bad. People had more compassion towards me being homeless with a baby.

Babies make people all mushy and make everyone's heart melt.

My aunt that lived across the bridge, had 3 sons. She was the first single woman that I had the pleasure of picking her brain. She was not married or dating at the time just working on getting her life together. We had lots of opportunities to just talk about life. Man, I was so comfortable at her house, we would stay up for hours and just talk about life. She wanted to be a beautician and become a business owner. She was probably the first woman that I ever conversed with about being a black woman and owning something. I did not know at that moment what business I wanted to own.

Just know I needed to be a business owner because that is where the money was at. I didn't really have time to focus on my dreams and goals, still trying to find my way. Helping children somehow who found themselves in similar predicaments was an idea I often pondered on.

Maybe I could have provided a place for homeless teenagers to live. There were so many possibilities and there were honestly many things I could do.

The sky was the limit, just didn't believe in me to push me the way I needed to be pushed. Boy do I miss the long conversations we had, she always told me to never give up. We talked so much about how hard the struggle was for black women trying to reach accomplishments on their own. Society is such a screwed-up place, so sad that these are issues facing American women. Especially women who looked like me.

I loved her energy and thrive for life, she never seemed to need a man. Independent! This was inspiring because almost every woman I knew was stressing over a man or he was stressing over her. To me, that was a level I wanted to be on but was so far, away from.

Because so many people missed me, I bounced from place to place. It was not a stressful kind of situation, this time everyone was concerned about what was going on with me. The only connection to me from anyone was my sister. Not sure what she told them, but they genuinely missed seeing me I believe. A lot of the women that took to me back home were older. Can't figure out why I attached to older women, but I needed them and their knowledge. I needed a compass and I genuinely used older people to create it.

Just seemed as if they were more experienced and had a different outlook on life. Wisdom is what I longed for was Wisdom was beautiful and I wanted to thrive in it. So, when I was in the presence of older women, I was always observing and learning. In the state of Delaware, I had family from the top to the bottom of the state. So, I just went where I was accepted with my child and where I felt I could make it. In three years, I had lived probably 25 different places from the age of 16-17. Here, there and everywhere. There were good and bad; negative and positive results caused by this action.

I did not keep a lot of material possessions because a lot of times I had to get up and go so everyday material possessions became less important to me. Surviving and survival were the number 1 factors in my life. If I could survive and finally get to that place in life I needed to be. Well, I was just going to SOUR! It's hard to keep up with clothes and important papers hopping from one house to the next. I also find it awfully hard to get comfortable anywhere. Not sure if I get bored easily or what the situation may be like as an adult, I still find it hard to get comfortable especially when there are too many variables. What I do know is that being kicked out of my mother and stepdad's home had a huge impact on my life.

It's ridiculously hard for me to trust people. Men nor women, it's not gender-specific, just people-related. I always felt like if your own mom doesn't like you, you were good for nothing.

For years I believed this lie. I believed tons of lies and untruths about me. Lies and fears that's what was holding me back from doing great things. Could be holding you back from being great things as well. Some of these lies can end up destroying us if we allow them to.

When you believe negative lies about yourself you begin to crumble. You can and you must overcome your past, it was and remains the hardest thing I ever had to do in my life. Altogether, it was worth it, and I am grateful and humbled at the same time. Me, you, us all, have a past that we must let go of. We just need to be active in the present working toward the future. I am so happy that I did not allow the lies to ruin my chances of being great.

My self-esteem was bad leading to a weird outlook on life. Yes, I had goals, dreams even talents. I didn't use any of them, there was no time to focus on me. Multitasking was nothing for me always reading so I was always striving for self-elevation, looking for like energies. People say many things but when you are a kid with no place to call home,

you watch everybody and everything, you're constantly in your head. Yeah, you might fight with people, but the fight with yourself is the biggest fight any of us will ever encounter. The biggest fight of your life. I would be back in forth in my head one minute I was ok the next minute emotions all over the place. How do you separate emotions from all these situations? Not that I can't answer, how I was coping at that moment, I just can't say. Was I coping, existing maybe, but I would not wish that life on my enemy?

Most of my energy went to making sure I could survive and find a place to rest my head.

When it was just me, I just talked to myself, sounds weird. I did though long nights walking all alone I would just pray for a better life.

To me everything happens for a reason, nothing happens by chance and sometimes not my choice.

What I would do if I actually had enough money to take care of me. Well for starters id tell my story then I would get myself a house. To this day as I write this book, I still feel fear that I could be kicked out or put out, so I can't wait to own my own home. Then great living will begin. In my books, I would tell what happened to me. Maybe even write a play about my life and my homegirls as teenagers. I could direct it in my own production studio with the assistance of a famous and great movie production team. I had to just for the cause.

I'd fight for rape victims and provide housing for single moms. Others had things going on in their life that had to be worse than mine. I help provide housing for addicts seeking help taking responsibility for their actions and wanting to do better.

For the most part, I was in my right mind and if I was crazy it had to help. I would be a boss and provide jobs for my community. Help single fathers provide and manage life and children. Feed the homeless and just help the world be a better place. The future looks so bright, I had to make it by any means necessary.

I just had to survive, me by myself with no one else. It was just me against the world, I had to prevail. This was my fight and like David and Goliath, just needed to find my correct weapon of war.

People can be so negative not all people just a lot. They are totally like crabs in a bucket watching for you to fall. They are like I didn't push you down, you didn't stop my fall either. Like I said not all people fit that description.

Some people are positive, full of life and are winning and want you to win. They inspire and provoke you to be more and want more. Those are the people you need to mimic and follow. Those that wanted me to fail so badly, I wanted to prove them wrong. Not me, I was not another statistic, not just a pushover. Some of the lessons the streets taught me I could not have learned anywhere else. The lessons that I was learning could have only been taught in specific ways.

Not saying I needed to go through all things thing to know better. There were lessons I learned just because I was in the wrong place at the right time. Learning was everywhere not just through my own personal experiences.

Learning not to judge anyone regardless of what they look like or taking people for granted. Valuable lessons that people could not have taught me. Waste not, want not, living in the moment.

I was no different from the next human that lived on the face of the Earth. My response would be everything though, I will show them all I am great. They wanted to see me in jail or on drugs. Watch me prove them wrong. My life will be a help for people great and small. Me the skinny kid who dressed funny and had the babies. I will not stop until I win. Life tried to swallow me up whole, but I made it even though life threw me up and spit me out. If nobody fights for me, I fight for me.

Yeah,

I'm not just special, I am pretty darn amazing.

HEALING

This is a story about a period in my life from 1991 to 1993.

The events and situations that I faced at the age of 16, 17 & 18. Being a teenager in America fighting every day to survive, wasn't easy. Definitely not a walk in the park.

However, my life was full of adventure, ups, and downs. You know the good, bad and ugly. I know you are all wondering how this story will officially end. You will just have to stay tuned to my site to see how this series will end. By then you will have traveled with me for almost 3 years.

The fact that I am still here alive in my correct mental state, is a tremendous blessing. I would be lying if I said I was not scared at times, but I could not just give up that was way too easy. Me and easy did not have a history so I needed a challenge even if I had to be the challenge.

This story will continue in my next book so I as always,

I continue to

hope anyone reading this book will find it as a source of healing for any situations that they face in their life. Whether it be abuse, rape, rejection, loneliness, depression. I care for humans across the globe. It is better for you and your health when you have healthier relationships. My desire is for people to Heal. I know there will always be problems for us to find solutions to.

None of us can take all the pain or hurt from our lives. Just real life where good and bad actually exist. I do not want you to see me, or you continue to go through cycles of hurt and abuse. If you are being abused REPORT, it. Get HELP for yourself, seek counseling. Not just seek it incorporate a healthy lifestyle. Healthy relationships, friendships, and healthy work relationships. Giving up is the easy way out, we all can't just give up? It is so much harder to fight for love, happiness, peace, and tranquility.

When we continue in anger, unforgiveness, and bitterness we draw the gun on ourselves. You can't give out negative energy and assume positive energy is going to come back. Not how things work in life, life is a boomerang, really what you send out will come back.

***Try hard to get rid of Fear it is a crippler. Do not be afraid to heal, grow and love.**

Yes, it makes us way too vulnerable at times. But I don't think a little vulnerability is all that bad. Some people look at being vulnerable as a weakness, I know I did. Being vulnerable is not about being weak at all. It's not about winning or losing. However, it's about having the courage to show up and be seen even when we have no control, or we are fearful or afraid. We all have different levels of vulnerability that we wrestle with.

When you try to shield or protect yourself from getting hurt. You do not allow for the intimacy of close relationships. Yes, it is hard to share your innermost thoughts and feelings with others. Especially when you don't want to experience more rejection. We as people must make a conscious decision to not hide our emotions from others. Freely express your thoughts, desires, and feelings regardless of what others do or say. If we try to resist all hazards and disasters that come into our life, we will look silly.

Trouble will come and still, the sun will shine. When you have a fear of rejection you keep your guards high. You do not allow others to see the real you. It's a constant struggle to fight against instinct, however, **Vulnerability is not our enemy**.

Most fear that if I express my insecurities or flaws that another may change their mind about what they perceive about me. We don't want to be misunderstood, mistreated, or abandoned.

This all has to do with our upbringings and how we were raised.

If parents encouraged, you to express yourself you probably connect well with others. Were as people like me had horrible connections with others. I showed vulnerability at an early age in life. So, when I got hurt, I struggled to open more around others. I take my time with these issues and ease into them instead of rushing in to change.

When I heal, I like to know why I respond in such a way and what would have been a better way for me to respond. For the most part, I don't like to repeat lessons. Paying attention to what is going on in and around you will help you take back control. The more you avoid your emotions or suppress them you lose sight of your true feelings. I rather fix or solve a problem than continue to let it fester without understanding.

Look at your life, find the problems you see, and work to correct them. When people bring things to your attention. Do not be so quick to get defensive and try to understand what they are saying. You may or may not agree but give them the respect and understanding you yourself would want. Listen to understand not respond.

We cannot change until we are willing to put in the work. This putting in work requires a bit of vulnerability, so you can't escape, that's so funny.

I have a great love for mother-daughter relationships. Daughters reflect their mom for the most part. Yes, we have our own identity, but you and your circle are who little girls imitate. We just must do better as women, we must want to *heal*.

Be a little more patient and gentler it's ok to not assume the worst. Good can happen, it does happen, and it will happen for you. For me, for us as people, the future is getting brighter! Of course, you can be bitter or angry but that prolongs the healing process. Like why resist the need to grow, to learn.

Be honest with yourself and see your own faults.

Yes, you could be getting hurt by those around you, but what are you doing to change the situation for yourself.

Dad's do you care? I do not judge; I'm just not convinced.

Absent parents where you at what is your excuse and why do you have so many? Stop being lazy, your children need you and your wisdom.

Women are not the only emotional creatures.

You guys can hold some grudges at your baby's mom's and vice versa. What does that solve, just wasted freaking time?

Life is so short but a vapor, here today, gone tomorrow. Not quotes, indeed a real fact.

I desire to have fathers open their hearts and mind to love.

Do not just walk away from a situation that you could have doubts about.

If you think you have a child with a woman be involved, a willing participant in your child's life.

Get on somebodies' nerves, somewhere.

Do not just walk away from these babies and be so heartless. I can never understand that with dudes, hide feelings for what. Not saying you have to be crying and stuff but what exactly is hiding your feelings doing for you? Are you living a longer life because of it or a stress-free life?

Does that make you a man to not show emotion?

To not wear your heart on your sleeve. Why are these even factors? If I were a dude any chick where my dick was, I feel would be suspect.

If my dick is in the vagina the pussy...Um should there be a question about whose baby it is? I'm bombarding you and your new boyfriend there would be three at every doctor's appointment because I would want to be involved. I get she could have fucked 6 more dudes that night. Not my problem, pick a better woman to date. Nobody told you to chase Juicy, now you are wondering if you could be the Pappy. I'd find out if I had made a baby or not, even if I had to inquire from friends and family.

I would not live comfortably knowing my seed from my dick was lost without a paddle. Just me my feelings and opinions don't beat my head off. These are just my thoughts.

But do not just walk away and leave a part of you all alone and lonely.

Let a mom, sister brother uncle someone pick up the slack and be there but don't leave these babies alone.

Someone must care; sure, kids act tough like they don't care. See past that hard shell, my shell was thicker than a tortoise.

On the inside, if you could ever get that far, I was soft as cotton.

In 1991,

*I had so many **Questions**.*

***Why better yet how**, was all this happening.*

*My **Background** started kind of rough.*

*Mostly, because **Hurt People Hurt**.*

*I went from feeling I had **NO Purpose***

*to understanding my purpose. We all know Living in **Toxic Situations***

can be a blinder for anyone. Causing situations to be Sadder

*than usual. Leaving one to feel as if they are the **Sacrificial Lamb**.*

*Left all alone growing up in the **City Life** changed me forever.*

*Forever, **Life will never be the Same**.*

*There were all sorts of **Choices and decisions**,*

*I just wanted to be a good person. I thought if I **Suppressed** my **feel-***

***ings**.*

It would make things better. That did nothing but turned me into a

Wandering Soul

*with **No place to call Home**.*

*I wanted to get away and I **Gotta getaway**.*

*I even traveled to **California**.*

*Yeah, it was tumultuous **Back and forth** but nothing a little **Healing** could not help!*

Fathers, you are needed more than you could know. A child needs a mother and a father regardless of what we say. Daughters need daddy too.

We must deal with moms that are imperfect every day. No man, no woman, no human is perfect. The same way moms fought daddies can too. Never should we pull out a scale and measure one's sin. Or attempt to pass judgment on another and not want it brought upon oneself, so very selfish.

Mothers and Fathers are not allowed to decide who is fit to be in a child's life. Especially based on past experiences and faults. Unless one is on a registry for child offenses or proven guilty in a court of law. We have no place making a decision so important that will affect another human's growth. No person has the right to hurt you.

What you put out comes back.

Moms get help go to counseling if you need to.

Family if you see that your family members have faults, and you don't try to address them. You are at fault to me. Unless the person is mentally unstable is the only reason, I would see not be real with a person. *Other than that people do better!*

Sitting back watching things thinking not talking about abuse is not helping a situation. For sure that cannot be the answer that you guys have come to about these types of situations.

We have no control sometimes over situations when it comes to family. However, when you know better you do better! You don't just sit around, and watch people hurt and know they need help. What is this so-called love word?

You all use it so effortlessly. Nope, love would not sit back and allow lies to rule any situation. Just because your hurt. Do not keep children, out of their dad's lives. Children can adapt to any situation they just copy what they see. Women need to stop being jealous of other women, I'm sick of the excuses, Sis just do better get up off your butt!

Everyone is avoiding pain; but do you pay attention that you are a causer of pain as well?

Yes, stepparents are amazing they can't be trying to be friends, though, and play both sides. My ex did this with my children and I didn't like it then and I don't like it now. You are a parent first and that holds a lot of weight. friends later and if you are going to be manipulative and cause pain just move on with your sorry self. When you become a stepparent, you can't be too mean, and you can't be too soft either. If you don't want the responsibility of children, don't date a person who has kids. There is a lane for every situation on Earth!

Stepparents have to stand firm as a parent in their strength and love.

So of course, you as a stepparent want to be loved from both sides. Do not, I repeat do not play both sides of the fence. Do not allow a person you are with to disregard a child's feelings. You may not know and that is just the simple truth. When you gain knowledge about anything you are held to that. When I learn not to steal, and I commit robbery I must be held accountable for my actions. Get help with your bitterness, resentment, anger, rage, and desire for revenge. For the record just because a stepparent is good to a child does not stop feelings of rejection or loneliness.

Stepparents are not the fixer-upper or all-time healer, do not put that weight there. Stepparents are not replacement parents. Some children just are blessed with 2 moms and 2 dads. Regardless of who is there, you are teaching someone. You have a great influence over the lives looking up to you. They have not no idea that you are there because you love them or not. So, it's up to up to you to care. Don't get in the way of child-parent relationships.

You should want the father, mother absent parent to be available. For children, absence and presence can both be positive and negative. That is why it takes a village to take care of us all. None of us have arrived or will ever arrive at the point that we need no-one. Humble yourself, or life will most definitely give you a humbling experience. It might have already done so you are just stubborn.

We all have sinned and come short; I believe that wholeheartedly. We do not have the right to pass judgment one to another. Judges when I tell you they have a hell of a job. Would never want to be in their shoes. If you feel unsafe go to the courts use the recourses that are available to you. To not would just be stuck in a cycle of abnormality.

To not want to change, grow or heal. That is a mental health issue. There are jobs of psychiatrist, counselor, guidance counselors, use the resources in your communities. If you are ever violated report the shit! Period point-blank! Don't stop keep moving! Give no voice to excuse, move stretch and grow! Surround yourself amongst people who have similar ideas and options.

Do not confuse things, my Stepdad was amazing in some ways and not well in others. Why because he was and is human. So were me and my mom humans. There are no books that teach us these things every situation is trial and error. Life is real and sometimes there are connections, other times some parents force connections. Some do not even ever feel each other, no connection, and ok no problem.

The only task that you are given is to love, care for and protect. We as humans use the skills that we were taught to the best of our ability. Then there are those of us who don't care, and well let's stick around and see if that is working well for them or not.

Simply different strokes for different folks.

These are real situations I beg people get help if they have mental issues. You should not feel embarrassed to get help for your problems. I believe that would be self-love. *Who cares what people think, you just have to be their dads! The same goes for moms just be there!*

BE RESPONSIBLE FOR THE LIFE YOU CREATE!

If it is too much to bear take a break, a vacation a message session, something.

Do better. All of us that can do better should do better. To turn a blind eye is a very selfish type of behavior.

NO! We can't save everyone, no matter how hard we try.

Having the mindset to be a part of the solution instead of the problem, might be a start. Some situations do require silence but only when protecting someone not when you are hurting them. Men and women stop with this domestic stuff. How is helping the one you hurt love. I keep forgetting a lot of these situations are not gender-specific. Some things men and women do alike, there just hidden.

That is cowardly to me, just my personal opinion. We must strive always for perfection. When we aim higher, we eventually get higher. Nothing in this life is free, but a headache. Everything else you must work hard for and keep at it. The key is to never give up on you to walk in excellence. Yes, you will fall I fall every day. I am the most imperfect person on earth you will find, daily I do things wrong I walk well in my Humanness.

Sometimes I make bad decisions, my words I choose may hurt someone. Without knowing I am doing something wrong to offend. So, I am no longer trying to be perfect I like being just who I am imperfection and all.

In my closing, I am thankful for everything I went through in life. I am who I am today because of my past. Just had to begin to understand me and the world we live in. I hold no ill will towards my Father, my Mother, or my Stepdad. I do not judge them for how they raised me. Just blessed that I survived and continue to move forward. I forgive them all and hold no animosity. These are my life events and who knows my story might even help someone. Might be you. I am alive and well.

Living and learning taking it one day at a time. At this point in my life, I am not a real religious person. I don't really get into conversations about religion or politics. Conversations with those topics are just not for me.

I do not profess to be any religion currently. The reason I am saying all this is because I grew up in the church. I love music in all genres and gospel being one of my favorites. Gospel artists speak about a lot of matters of the heart and how we are to uphold ourselves.

Worship which is my favorite gospel music is kind of passionate.

I was 14,15 and 16 my way of escape would come through music most times. When I put music on, I just seem to get lost in the magic of the feeling.

One of the songs that I would sing as a child.

Whenever I was alone, and or needed encouragement I would sing this song. I love you all be Blessed! Smooches!

The artist was a gospel artist named

Zella Jackson Price.

And the lyrics are as follows

> I may not be the best at anything
> or have the best of anything
> sometimes I feel like I'm the least of all but
> I know someone
> who has everything?

and
he is my everything and I'm
happy just to know that I'm his child
His name is Jesus the righteous son of God
lily of the valley bright and morning
star his name is Jesus
and he's my everything
and I am happy
just to know that I'm his child

Born Raylene Young,
To Allen K. Hayman and Ivory & Barry Williams, Raylene began to
write as an outlet of expression.   Her books
are encouraged for women and men as well.
Her writings make you think from a different perspective. As a
means of expressing herself, Raylene began to write about events and
problems she faced growing up in a dysfunctional family. She talks about
issues that people don't want to discuss.
Topics like rape, abuse, and trauma. Mental illness and domestic violence just to name a few.

Writing became an outlet for her to express her feelings and
Also, help her reach her dream of becoming a famous author.
As an Emotional Writer, Raylene writes material that establishes
something meaningful between her and her readers.
As most of her writing, are about a life event. She expresses her art
through Self-help and Motivational books. Both fiction and non-fiction
novels. From time to time she may do a collaboration of poems. Healing
and the sanity of man is some of her favorite topics to discuss.
Her biggest motivation has been her children and the hopes of a better you better me.

In
other
wordz
Publishing